Adventures in Christianity

Lessons in Fearless Living Through an Unfailing God!

Who says it is not exciting to be a Christian?

Casey Hawley
Atlanta, GA

Dedication

This book is dedicated to God who is my loving, generous, and all-powerful Father, Jesus who is my brother, friend, and advocate, and the Holy Spirit who guides me, prompts me, goes before me, and shows me which way to turn when I am clueless.

For I know the plans I have for you," declares the LORD, "plans to prosper you and not to harm you, plans to give you hope and a future.
Jeremiah 29:11

Marginal footer

Adventures in Christianity

*Lessons in Fearless Living Through an Unfailing God
Who Says It Is Not Exciting to Be a Christian?*

ઠ

INTRODUCTION ❧

I used to think being a Christian would be boring. That was just one of the many reasons I did not want to be one. No one was more surprised than I was when at thirty-eight, I found I could no longer deny the reality of God. When you come to know God, really know Him personally, He requires that you acknowledge His son Jesus. That meant I had to be a Christian, and though I knew I must since God was undeniable to me, I was not excited about living a Christian lifestyle. I thought the exciting life I had led was over. And my old life **was** over, but a new one began that was far more exciting than anything I could ever have imagined for myself.

That is why I am writing this book. I want people who are hesitating to open their minds to Jesus as I did for so many years to know that life as a Christian is dynamic. Having the power of the Living God and Jesus Christ at your side as you walk through life is like walking through life as a superhero—except you are not the hero. He is. His power is yours as you face every challenge life inevitably throws at you.

...In this world you will have trouble. But take heart! I have overcome the world." John 16:33

Jesus never promised us we would not have trouble; in fact, He told us the opposite, that we should expect trouble in this world. I think we can agree He is right. No one goes through this life unscathed. Your experience may be that you have been faced with financial difficulties or health problems or relationship problems. Some people seem to be hit with all of these challenges, meant to discourage.

But Jesus also says we have reason to take heart! He has already overcome every challenge we face, if we believe in Him and turn our problems over to Him to solve them His way. No one says it will be fast or easy in the meantime, but the victory is assured. We can be confident in that.

This book is also for Christians who have known Him for a very long time. Take heart! If you have become discouraged and worn down by life, remember the power of God is yours as His beloved child. The same power that resurrected Jesus can renew your strength, untangle your messes, and defeat whatever is coming against you. These events on the following pages are just some of the ways God gave me tangible help in extremely difficult circumstances. What He did for me is available to everyone who believes and calls on Him. He did this for us, according to the book of Hebrews 6:18-19, to give us hope and make us secure in an unsure world:

God did this so that, by two unchangeable things in which it is impossible for God to lie, we who have fled to take hold of the hope set before us may be greatly encouraged. We have this hope as an anchor for the soul, firm and secure…

The Bible tells those who believe to "fear not" 365 times. Over and over through the thousands of years its many authors wrote this bestseller, the message was the same: Do not fear! Fear not! Fear no evil!

What keeps you up at night? What is the one grief or regret of your life? God can take this on for you, and the amazing thing is that He wants to. He longs to take this burden off you and put it on His very capable shoulders. Please read this book with expectation. It is in your hands for a reason. Put away cynicism, skepticism, and weariness. Allow God to show you what it is He wants to show you about how He works and Who He is.

X

I. ⁊ God Is With You When You Are Outnumbered

One of the great thrills of my life was in August of 2001 when a friend recommended me to do some writing for a brochure for the Billy Graham Training Organization. She had been interviewing for a job there and realized that she was not a fit for the position presented to her. She interrupted her interview and said to the interviewer, "I apologize, but I would not be the right person for this job, and I don't want to take more of your very stretched time to proceed." The executive doing the interviewing then relaxed and said how much he appreciated her honesty. He said, "It is not urgent that I place someone in this job. What I urgently need is a writer."

My friend said, "Would you like for me to recommend a writing contractor to help you while you search?"

The executive said "yes" and called me right away. I went for a half-day meeting with the executive and some of his team. My heart was so encouraged to find that this fine organization was authentically Christ-like—just as much behind the scenes as in public. Everyone I met wanted to do God's work God's way. Most had given up lucrative jobs in marketing or as C-level executives to serve in Billy Graham's efforts to win souls to Christ and to equip pastors in villages and cities all over the world to teach and to preach.

The team decided I would start on my first assignment a couple of weeks later, but that was not to be. On September 11, 2001, the twin towers of The World Trade Center were destroyed, and the tragedy of 2,997 lost lives rocked our nation. Grief for the families and for the victims was deep, and people wanted to help. I was so proud of our nation as donations poured into the Red Cross to help those affected by the death and destruction.

Other charities understood that for a time, donations needed to go to this important cause, and for about a year, donations to most other non-profits were lower than had been projected. In that time, the project I had been scheduled to work on for the Billy Graham organization was canceled.

Much to my surprise, I got a call about a month after the cancellation from the executive who had interviewed me initially. He said, "Can you get up here tomorrow? We now have funding for the brochure and would like to meet with you first thing in the morning."

Normally, I would have said, "Impossible!" for two reasons. First, I rarely traveled on school nights during the time I was raising my son, who was twelve at the time. Second, I would need to leave that day to be there in time for an early morning meeting since Asheville was four hours away. As a single mom, finding a good sleepover solution for my son on short notice was my first hurdle, not to mention packing and clearing my appointment calendar for the necessary two days.

More of a concern to me was that I was going to have to violate another personal rule of mine. I have been a consultant on business writing and communication for many years and had traveled a great deal before my son was born. My sometimes unpleasant experiences of arriving in urban areas late at night and not always finding safe parking had led to my creating a rule for myself: I always scheduled myself to arrive at my destination by

3:00PM in the afternoon. Even with flight delays, slow traffic and other glitches, this policy offered me some protection against arriving at midnight in an unsafe, unfamiliar area. I was a woman of many fears in those days, and the fear of being attacked while traveling alone topped my list. I had taken every self-defense course for traveling women I could find and avoided travel if at all possible.

But this opportunity was an exception. I agreed to go, and set about making the myriad arrangements needed for a single mom with a small business. By the time I left Atlanta, rush hour traffic had started, and it took me six hours to make the drive to Asheville. I used my cell en route to make a hotel arrangement, but all the familiar hotels were booked due to a local event. I finally found a budget motel I had never heard of but that was close to my destination.

When I arrived at about 11:00PM, I saw a sketchy motel with a strange configuration. As I pulled in from the highway, I saw two buildings that looked like giant concrete blocks, three stories high. They sat side by side. To the far right of one of the buildings was a tiny house where guests checked in. I drove up to the little house, woke the night clerk and checked in with great regret that I had not been able to reserve a better hotel on short notice. But I was tired and the motel was convenient, so I shook off my uneasiness and decided this place would do fine for one night's sleep. As I drove away from the tiny house and looked at the first blocky building in the pitch dark, I at first thought that no one was out except me. Good, I thought. All is quiet. At the front of these buildings was the highway. At the back were thousands of acres of deep dark woods, ascending toward a huge mountain that loomed in the distance.

As I rounded the corner and started to drive up the hill between the two tall buildings, I saw near the highway an old, dusty, brown station wagon in the first parking space on my left. I saw one man crouched in the back of the station wagon working with something, though I could not see exactly what. A second very large man was standing at the back of the station wagon, doing nothing but looking around the parking lot. He looked exactly like the character from the Popeye cartoons called Bluto—muscular, black stubbly beard, and pasty white skin that looked as if he had not seen daylight for a while. I found out later how accurate that was.

As my apprehension mounted, I told myself, "Don't be such a coward and so apprehensive. They are just like you. They are just unpacking their belongings and settling in— no need for concern."

My room was on the right, closer to the back of the building, so I pulled into my space and prepared to exit the car and get to my room as fast as possible. I put my laptop strap over one shoulder along with my purse and walked to the back of the car to get my overnight bag. As I strapped my overnight bag over my other shoulder and closed the trunk, I looked up to see Bluto walking toward me. He was still about fifteen yards away and walking slowly, but he was definitely approaching me. As he walked toward me, I realized that there was no ice machine or soft drink machine in my direction nor any other good reason he would walk towards me and the deep, dark woods.

As he walked, he was talking nonsense in an eerily calm voice, as if he were trying to soothe me. He told me, "Yes, my friend and I have been all over three counties tonight. We got into a little scrape not far from here. Then we had dinner." He seemed not to care what he said but to be determined to keep talking in that low, hypnotic voice while he slowly advanced toward me. It reminded me of the Horse Whisperer, yet I was the animal he was trying to calm. When he got within about ten yards, I realized that despite all my rationalizations for why he was approaching me, that he was about to do me great harm. I had been saying scriptures to myself and to the Lord in my head like, "I can do all things through Christ who strengtheneth me" and all the "Fear not" verses I could remember. But suddenly, I felt the panic uncontrollably welling up in me, and I shot up an arrow prayer to the Lord. "Oh Lord," I cried in my spirit, "I know I am not supposed to live in fear, but Lord, there are TWO of them!"

I cannot explain what happened next. I did not hear an audible voice, but I clearly heard God say in my heart, "Yes, and there are two of *us*."

No earthly person has ever been as real to me as God was in that parking lot in that moment. In fact, I was so aware of His presence as He reminded me there were two of us that I almost burst out laughing at the thought of how puny Bluto was compared to the power of God. Yes, this muscle-bound man was huge, but up against the God of the universe, he was powerless. I was part of a two-person team and the other person had created that mountain behind me, could slay armies of armed soldiers, and could turn the ocean tides. I went from being a puddle of fear to being completely confident.

I remembered what my self-defense courses had taught me: "When overpowered or outnumbered, hand over your purse and give the attacker whatever he wants. Don't antagonize or challenge him. Be submissive." But instead, I heard myself saying with great authority, "What do you want?"

Bluto said, "I want money."

I said, "I will give you money if you turn and walk away, but if you come one step closer, I will not give you a penny."

Bluto put his hands up in a soothing way and took two baby steps to the right and said, "Okay, okay," in his best Horse-Whisperer manner. A decent man would have walked away, but he simply went to the side. Later, a district attorney told me he was trying to get on my side because the most effective take down method is not from the front or back but from the side. He was positioning himself to take me down in a way I would be rendered defenseless. However, when he took those two steps to the right, I knew that there was never going to be a better moment to make a break for it.

And then God told me to run. I knew that the laws of physics and the natural would say there was no way I could get back around to the side of my car, open the door and get away as laden down as I was with two bags and a laptop, but I ran anyway. My greatest concern was getting the key in the ignition in the dark with shaky hands. My entire focus was on opening the car door and getting the key into that tiny slot. But I knew for sure that I was supposed to do that very thing. I also knew for sure that if I didn't, this bad situation was about to get much, much worse.

With God's grace, I somehow escaped Bluto. It made no earthly sense that I made it to my car ahead of him, but it happened. It reminded me of when Jesus was hidden from the people of Nazareth who had dragged Him to a cliff and were about to throw him off, but He simply slipped through the crowd as if He were unseen and got away. (Luke 4:30) As I drove quickly through the parking lot toward the highway, I looked to my right and into the back of the dusty brown station wagon. I finally saw what Bluto's partner was doing. He was spreading out a canvas tarp in the flat back area of the station wagon. They had been hunting, hunting for a woman as some might hunt for a deer.

I later was told that Bluto had been released from prison just days ago and was a violent career criminal. At the time, I just knew I had escaped from an experience of pure evil. I drove away from the motel as fast as I could, but then the picture of that tarp being spread would not leave my mind. They were not finished.

The two men had not captured me, but they were out for a night of hunting and would move on to another prey. I called 911, but because I had traveled about three miles, I was in a different jurisdiction from where the motel was. They told me to call Asheville police. The Asheville police told me that was not their jurisdiction and to call the state patrol. In all, I contacted five numbers. And there was another reason no one wanted to take my report: Nothing had happened to me. Thanks to my God who knows every hair on my head and who cares for me, I had not been robbed, beaten or raped.

When I called that fifth number, I was trembling from the exhaustion of my ordeal and, unfortunately, lost my temper. I said. "I know you don't want to take my report but I insist you take it anyway. You know the local police departments around here; I don't. I am telling you that these men are going to hurt someone tonight if you don't do something fast. I am not going to call anyone else tonight. If you don't find the correct agency to find these men before they capture another woman, it is on you."

The person on the other end of the line said lazily, "Alright." As I gave my report, I had visions of the person surfing the net while I talked instead of writing down my report, but I needed to find a someone to turn this over to someone and get sleep before I dropped.

We had a productive meeting at the Billy Graham Training Center the next morning, and I saw no reason to share what had happened. I wondered if one of the law enforcement agencies would try to contact me, but they didn't-- not for about five months.

One afternoon while I was working in my home office, I received a call from a police department in a small town in North Carolina I had never heard of. The officer said, "Are you Casey Hawley, and were you in the vicinity of Asheville, NC on October 4, 2001?"

I said yes and he said, "We need to come see you." My heart froze. For a fleeting second I wondered if this might be Bluto who had tracked me down through my tag number. Noting my hesitation, the officer very kindly said, "Would you feel better if we asked one of your local policemen to interview you?" I agreed and someone came to my home within the hour.

The seasoned police officer doing my interview asked me to start at the beginning and tell everything. Since this was an official police report, I did not tell everything, leaving out the part about my arrow prayer and how God spoke to me so clearly that night. When I got to the end of my very objective recitation of the facts, he looked at me solemnly for a long time. Finally, the police officer said, "Ma'am, it could only have been the grace of God that allowed you to escape. These are two of the most violent offenders in North Carolina, with a history of attempted murder, rape and all sorts of violence. Now tell me again how you got away."

Then I told him the real story about my prayer and how God plucked me out of that parking lot against all odds. Even though he was a believer, he still could not believe I got away. Only the God of the impossible could have made my escape possible.

Finally, he told me that within one hour and within a mile-and-a-half of that budget hotel, the two men had allegedly kidnapped a woman who has never been heard from again. The police found her dental plate by the side of the road where she had been walking. She had had a fight with her husband and had gotten out of his car and decided to walk home.

She was assumed dead and there were several clues that pointed to the two men who had accosted me. My testimony, however, would be the final evidence needed to convict them with circumstantial evidence. I never had to go to trial as they worked out a plea deal.

I don't know why God decided to spare my life that night but not the life of the other woman. Maybe the purpose was to share this story with you. I do know He has a plan and that our days are written down in Heaven as part of that plan that works for our good and for His glory. I also know that an amazing thing happened that night to me. I had been a woman consumed with fear of going to unknown places, especially when I traveled for business. From that moment forward, I have not been afraid to travel.

I also mourned the death of the other woman for a long time. Though I never met her, I felt a connection to her I cannot explain.

The extraordinary experience I had that night was such a personal encounter with the Lord that I could not talk about it for almost two years. I meditated on God's deliverance and I thanked Him often, but I did not tell anyone.

Finally, I have begun to tell this story to encourage others who are in impossible circumstances and need the God of the impossible to deliver them. Are you in need of encouragement today? God has these words for you:

- *Do not fear or be dismayed because of this great multitude, for the battle is not yours but God's. 2 Chronicles 20:15*
- *You need not fight in this battle, station yourselves, stand and see the salvation of The Lord on your behalf....Do not fear or be dismayed; tomorrow go out to face them for The Lord will go with you. 2 Chronicles 20:17*

Pray now that God will deliver you from your enemies as He delivered me from mine.

II. ❧ God Is With You in Danger

When my son was ten months old, my husband and I separated. We had separated many times before, but this time I sensed it was for good. Because I had earnestly sought the Lord and tried for years to avoid a divorce, I was crushed and felt such failure. As we worked out visitation for my precious baby and tried to hammer out a life that had departed from God's perfect plan for us, everything seemed surreal. I tried not to succumb to just wanting to curl up in my bed to cry all day. I had a baby to raise, and I knew that babies sense emotions and are influenced by events they are too young to understand. I determined to take care of myself for my son's sake.

I did pretty well in the daytime when I was either playing with my baby, doing some local seminars, or working from my home office. Staying busy helped. Though I read my Bible for hours before bedtime, the evenings were a bit harder as I had more time to think and reflect.

The evening came when I had to release my young son for his first overnight visit. Though he loved his son, my husband had always been vocal about not wanting to babysit even for a couple of hours, so I was concerned. I also could not bear to think about the possibility that my baby would wake in the night and want me and not understand that for the first night of his life that I was not there. My mind really wanted to go there.

So I made plans to go to a Christmas program at a local church. I felt that the praise and worship would get my mind on God and not on myself. It was a great plan while it lasted. The problem was that the program was at 6:30. Church musical programs I had attended in the past usually lasted at least two hours and often went overtime. Not this one. I was in my car and returning home by 7:30PM.

As I drove, I was overwhelmed with loneliness and could not bear the thoughts of going home to a house devoid of little baby noises and all the activity that usually filled my home. I thought, "I cannot go in there, but where can I go?" I was driving near a movie theater where my husband and I often went in the early years of our marriage. I realized I had not been to the movies since my baby was born. I decided to go see if a movie might be starting soon, and there was. I felt that if I could sit there and get my mind engaged in something besides this ache in the pit of my stomach, that I would be the better for it. I also felt that since it would be after 10:00PM when I got home, that I might just be able to go straight home and fall in bed without imagining all the things that might be going on with my child.

I watched the movie and congratulated myself on being brave enough to actually go to a movie by myself. It was not something I would ordinarily do, but this was not an ordinary night. I sat in the pitch dark of the movie theater and temporarily departed from my world and lived in the fantasy world of the actors for a while. This cinema complex was showing six movies in its six different theaters that night. When the movie was over, we all trudged out in the dim half-light of our theater. The minute we opened the doors to the well-lit lobby, we were greeted by a dozen men in black S.W.A.T. gear from head-to-toe. An assault rifle was pointed directly at me. If you have never had a fiercely intense man with an assault rifle grimly bearing down on you, let me assure you that it is terrifying. While they were aiming at the crowd exiting into the lobby, the S.W.A.T. team was screaming, "Get down! Get down on the ground!" "Get out of here." "Go through that door."

Now, I am not the most coordinated person in the best of circumstances. I was completely confounded by the instructions to get down on the floor yet to keep walking to exit the building. This made two of the S.W.A.T. team members yell even more loudly at me as I suppose they felt I was resisting. I looked around and saw some of my fellow-theater-goers duck-walking out the door. I got with the program then and did my best to follow suit, though a recent back surgery made this almost impossible and terribly painful.

More S.W.A.T. members yelled at us as we approached the door. "Single-file! No one leave!" When I went through the door, I immediately entered a world that was totally unlike anything I could ever imagine. A huge black S.W.A.T. helicopter was hovering as low over the parking lot as it could get. The police on board were watching every move we made. I saw that some of the police officers on board were looking down and around the parking lot. What were they looking for? Whom were they looking for? The sounds, the yelling, the black garb and gear, all looked like something from a big budget Bruce Willis movie and not a scene from my life.

As I was exiting the theater, the S.W.A.T. guys at the door of the theater motioned with their weapons for us to line up single file along a long wall outside the theater that went to the street. "Up against the wall!" they shouted. "Single file!" "Stay down!"

We still had no idea what was going on, but it was terrifying. When we first exited, we did not know if the people with guns on us were bad guys or police, though they appeared to be official police officers. We were helpless to do anything but follow the instructions of these men who were obviously serious about our obeying their commands.

We lined up, still squatting and keeping our heads down below the low wall. This was excruciating for me. I had experienced a great deal of damage to my back during childbirth and had been under the care of a neurologist; this position was definitely against doctor's orders. The position was quite painful for me to hold, but I never questioned the fact that I had to comply or suffer some severe consequences. I knew this was for our safety, but that did not make the position any less painful.

We were threatened and told not to use our cell phones. Each person was individually searched and questioned. It took a long time as everyone in our theater was in that line. When the interrogators did not find what they were looking for, they started over again at the front of the line. I was close to the end. By that time, some bold people had surreptitiously used their cell phones to call loved ones. I had no one to call except a baby who was in the care of a man who would not accept a call from me. He would think I was checking on him. The people who made calls passed along the information they had learned. Families at home knew more than we did because everything that was happening to us was being broadcast live on the 11:00 news. We were smack in the middle of a desperate hostage situation.

While we had been watching the movie, four men and one woman had allegedly come in and attempted to rob the theater. They had taken over the offices where the money was kept. At some point, something went terribly wrong, and a silent alarm brought the first team of police. We learned that while this robbery was going on upstairs, we theatergoers had been blissfully watching our movies with the volume turned up full blast.

The first police team on the scene was not prepared for five armed robbers, so two critical things set this nightmare in motion. Although the local police were able to capture three robbers, one took an office employee hostage. Another robber was able to slip away. Police had believed that the fifth robber had slipped into one of the theaters and mixed in with the crowd. They believed it was his plan to exit the theater posing as one of us theatergoers and leave the scene as if he were, like us, an innocent moviegoer. What we had been enduring had been the police officers' attempt to sift through the crowd and determine who was a violent criminal and who was a regular citizen out for what was supposed to be a very tame evening of taking in a movie.

While squatting there together, I struck up a friendship with a young couple. They had been part of the brave but rebellious souls who had secretly used their cell phones to find out what was going on since the police had still had not had time to share any information with us. Together we watched the scouring of the parking lot to find the lost robber. We saw probably a half dozen police officers rolling on their backs under cars to see if the robber was clinging to the undercarriage of someone's car. The search was very thorough. I can't express how kind this young couple was to me as we watched and waited for well over an hour and as my back pain from damaged nerves became more intense. My concern was that I felt I was reinjuring my back and that I would have to return to the hospital for surgery and leave my baby for a full week again.

The S.W.A.T. team on the inside continued to search the theater using the same methods they used on us. Movie endings were staggered. About every 15 minutes, a movie ended and a new line of movie-watchers left the darkness of their theater and were greeted by the screaming S.W.A.T. team members and their assault weapons. I am not complaining. I know I could have been taken hostage at some point if those guns had not been trained on every person who left the theater. Still, it was an experience that had left us all shaken and exhausted.

After all movies had ended and all theatergoers had been searched twice with no results, a rumor circulated through the crowd that the police might search everyone a third time. We waited another hour behind the wall, not knowing if we were free to go or not. There was no police officer near us to clarify whether we could leave as they all had seemed to return to the main parking lot to search. The young couple and I were at the end of the wall nearest the street. Then the kind young woman whispered to me, "We tried to call a taxi to leave, but all the streets near the theater are blocked off so the police can look for the robber."

I said, "I am going to pray." Now, normally, I am the most cooperative, law-abiding citizen imaginable. And when I prayed, I was not praying for a taxi. I was praying that God would deliver us out of this dangerous situation, but when my eyes opened, there was a taxi right in front of us, and the driver said to the young couple, "Did anyone here call a taxi?"

The young couple looked at me in disbelief and then bolted for the taxi, dragging me by the arm as we left. I would not have been surprised to hear bullets whizzing by as we departed, but I chose to believe optimistically that the searches were over as some of my new friends had said. We never could explain how that one taxi was allowed around the barricades and then was allowed to leave unhindered. All I know is that I was home in 15 minutes and was watching the people we had just left remain crouched and waiting for another hour.

The fifth robber was never found. Was he one of us behind the wall? Had he escaped during the first confusion when only a couple of police officers answered the first call? No one knows.

I do know that God brought me through a potentially dangerous situation without allowing harm to one hair on my head.

And though I did think that night about my sweet baby and what might happen if someone took me hostage or shot me, I will say that after my escape that for the rest of that night I was not sitting home counting the minutes and agonizing over hypothetical situations that could happen to my child. And when I finally finished watching my fellow movie-watchers on the news slowly trickle out of the parking lot, I was exhausted and had no trouble going to sleep!

God can extricate you from the most dangerous situations if you will pray, as we learn in Mark 11:23-25:

Truly I tell you, if anyone says to this mountain, 'Go, throw yourself into the sea,' and does not doubt in their heart but believes that what they say will happen, it will be done for them.

Therefore I tell you, whatever you ask for in prayer, believe that you have received it, and it will be yours. 25 And when you stand praying, if you hold anything against anyone, forgive them, so that your Father in heaven may forgive you your sins.

He cares about the big dangers, but He also cares about our smallest needs according to Luke 12:4-7:

I tell you, my friends, do not be afraid of those who kill the body and after that can do no more. 5 But I will show you whom you should fear: Fear him who, after your body has been killed, has authority to throw you into hell. Yes, I tell you, fear him. 6 Are not five sparrows sold for two pennies? Yet not one of them is forgotten by God. 7 Indeed, the very hairs of your head are all numbered. Don't be afraid; you are worth more than many sparrows.

Do you feel vulnerable or fearful about anything in your life? Your future, finances, relationships, or health? He cares. Pray to God, your Father, who wants to bless you and loves you even more than an earthly parent could ever love you. God is your loving Father, the only perfect parent that has ever lived.

III. ～ God Is With You in Rejection

I once had an amazing experience with God in a hospital corridor that left me surer that He cares tenderly for me than I could ever imagine. This experience came when I was feeling the deep pain of rejection and alienation from my family.

Let me first explain how much I love my sister Jan. Jan was eight years younger than I, and for much of her childhood my mother was quite ill and hospitalized for long periods of time. When I was thirteen and wanted to go to a Saturday morning football game at my junior high school or shopping at the mall with my friends, it was a package deal. My parents expected me to take Jan with me everywhere, as I was her de facto caregiver. Surprisingly, I not only didn't mind it but adored this little girl with all my heart. Probably half my babysitting money from our neighbors went to buy things for Jan as I delighted in seeing her face light up with joy. Though I was a child myself, I functioned as a third parent.

As we grew older, Jan developed drug and alcohol problems that sometimes strained her relationships with family members. She was also diagnosed as bipolar. Even my parents who loved her extravagantly had seasons when they had to set boundaries with Jan. In those times, my parents wanted me to try to maintain a relationship with Jan and to be the link to our family. I did, and Jan and I had some wonderful times together, in the midst of some very difficult times. I was the only family member who participated in all of the many rehab programs she participated in for over twenty years.

In 2007, my Jan came to me and said, "I have something to tell you. I have not told you this for almost a year because I knew you would make me go to the hospital." Jan knew I still had that big sister bossiness in me.

She said, "I have a lump larger than a lemon in my breast."

I said, "Well, you are right about one thing: I am going to make you go to the doctor."

She insisted on going to a doctor near her home in White, Georgia. I begged her to go to my doctor at the Breast Center, but she did not want to make the 35 minute drive. She went to a clinic near her where the doctor did not seem to realize the urgency of her situation. He never took x-rays and did not pursue investigating for cancer, even after several visits. After over a month of unproductive visits, I told her she should insist the doctor get x-rays. He sent her to the hospital in Marietta for the x-rays. At that time, the technician broke protocol and told her she had cancer. She asked him who was the best doctor around, and he told her that my doctor at the Breast Center would be his choice. With this unbiased recommendation, Jan proceeded to make an appointment. When I took her to see Dr. Philip Israel, he immediately pronounced she had Stage 4 breast cancer. In her subsequent surgery, we would find she also had 21 active lymph nodes. What proceeded next was the most ferocious battle against cancer I have ever witnessed. Her team included Dr. Israel, the oncologist Dr. Mike Andrews, and another surgeon, Dr. Bill Barber. She endured the harshest chemo and radiation. She had multiple surgeries. Often it seemed she was losing the battle, and the odds against her were great.

For six years, I was my sister's only consistent source of support during this battle. Jan was a charming and brilliant woman. She had several friends throughout those years who came and went, but I was the one person who was there for her throughout it all. I will never regret one moment of that time.

We walked through many rocky times together. I remember the day of my mother's funeral was especially difficult for Jan. She had gotten her feelings hurt with a family member and was distraught. Her chemo was at a critical juncture, but she called me on my cell as we left the graveside and said, "I am not going to get my chemo tomorrow. I am going to call the doctor and tell him I am quitting chemo. Why should I live if life is going to kick me in the teeth?"

I knew she was in a fight for her life, and that skipping chemo for even a week could be a fatal mistake.

I told her, "I understand why you might want to quit chemo and let nature take its course. And I will support you if you want to get some rest and make that decision in a few days. But that is not a decision you should make today. You are burying your mother. You are angry with someone else. Don't let your anger dictate an important decision like that."

She finally decided to get the next round of chemo and postpone the decision to end treatment for a week. After that week, she decided to see the treatment through to the end.

Miraculously, Jan went into remission. She slowly stopped being so terribly sick and she began to look more healthy and radiant than ever. She drew closer to the Lord and we had many wonderful talks about Him and His mercy and grace. She attended some church and women's events with me. She got a job as a restaurant reviewer for Yahoo, and we began to try many new restaurants together and had more fun than we had ever had. She lost her taste for alcohol, and life was the best for her it had ever been.

We were so excited because Jan was approaching a real milestone for a cancer survivor: her three-year anniversary of being cancer-free. Instead, at her appointment we thought would be a celebration, she found out that the cancer had returned.

That year was another difficult one. The cancer metastasized to the bones and her prognosis was not good. No chemo made a difference this time. It appeared that Jan did not have long to live. As we sat in the oncologist's office, Jan tried to get a projection of how long she had to live, but the doctor did not like to talk in terms of "expiration dates." From study information he shared, we figured she might have six months if some new chemo trial did not give her an antidote.

I had been scheduled to teach in Italy that summer for Georgia State University, but I canceled my trip. I knew I was letting down the dean, my teaching partner, and the students by asking someone else to take my place, but I knew I could not leave Jan.

I continued to be there to tempt her to eat and to keep her strength up. Again, her life expectancy seemed to be short. I took her to Florida twice and we made some wonderful memories as we middle-aged women played like children on the beach.

Then some friends from college found Jan after a long time of being out of touch. I cannot say enough appreciative things about these friends who began to treat her to lunch and trips to the beach at their luxurious beach homes, and encourage her in so many ways. I thank God they came back into her life. Jan's friend Susan was especially helpful and began to take Jan to all her doctor's appointments. I was especially glad because, after all, I was still the big sister. Jan did not want me to go on all her appointments, just the critical ones. She did not mind Susan's going, however, so I was glad.

For some reason I will never know, Jan at some point sent me a text that said, "Do not contact me, text me or email me." Nothing had happened to trigger this event. The last time I had seen her was when I had taken her out for her birthday lunch. She had called that night to say how much fun she had had and that the birthday gift I had given her was perfect. I was perplexed. With Jan, however, some periods of unpredictable behavior had happened before. I thought this hiatus in our relationship would be over soon as it always was, but the breach lasted for a couple of months. I would send her cards or drop off a meal at her door or text and tell her I love her and ask if she needed anything, but there was no response. The odd thing was that she would send me messages through other people that I had done nothing wrong and that she was not angry with me. Jan often had her own reasons for doing things like this that our family did not understand, and we had learned just to wait it out. The problem was, we did not have that much time left with Jan.

I became more concerned when I heard Jan had been given two to four weeks to live. She was in our local hospital having tests.

My plan was to go to the hospital and drop off some flowers, a card, and her favorite fancy deodorant that she loved as a splurge. I planned to leave these items at the nurse's station so as not to dishonor her wishes not to see me, but I wanted her to know I was there, physically there. I decided to consult my aunt who loves Jan very much and knows her well. I told her I wanted to go see Jan in the hospital, but that I did not want to force her to see me against her will. My aunt said, "People often say things like that when they are very sick. If it were my sister, I would go."

I prayed and prayed, asking God what I should do. I did not get my answer then. I finally said to God, "I don't know what your answer is, but I know you are not trying to hide anything from me." I said to Him, "I am going to go. If you don't want me to go, stop me."

I was blocks from the hospital when my sister Bobbi called. She said, "Casey, DON'T GO! Jan says that if you come, she will have you escorted off the premises by security." I felt this was God stopping me from intruding, but I felt clear direction (for the first time) that He wanted me to deliver the gifts and flowers to the nurse's station. I had been going to this same hospital to visit the sick for over 50 years; however, when I entered, I took a "wrong" turn and wound up on a hall of offices. A woman named Kamisha was walking down the hall and saw me looking at overhead signs and said, "Are you looking for something? May I help you?" I tried to keep my answers short because, quite honestly, what Bobbi had said made me want to just sit down and cry—a lot. What could be going on in Jan's very confused mind that would make her shut the door to the one person on earth who had loved her consistently and upheld her when no one else would? I told Kamisha that I did not know my sister's room number or how to get there. She said to come in her office and she would look it up for me. She continued to try to talk to me, but I was trying to stay quiet, as I was fighting back tears. She said, "Where are you from?" I said, "Marietta. Where are you from?" She said, "Villa Rica." I said I used to drive through there when I went to the University of West Georgia at night. She said that she went to West Georgia at night. We found so much we had in common. She found Jan's room number and then said, "You would have to walk around this entire hospital to get there from here. I am going to stop what I am doing and take you there by a shortcut."

I told her, "I know God sent you to meet me in that hallway today. I have had severe pain this week from a back injury and have vertigo from it today. I don't think I could have done that much walking." She said that every conversation is ordained. She gave me her testimony of her trials that had brought her to Kennestone Hospital. She had been working in Savannah in her specialty when she wanted to move back to the Atlanta area. Though she did not want to work in hospice, that was the only job available for her as a social worker. She praised the Lord for the training hospice gave her because her mother started dying the next year, and now Kamisha was trained and prepared for what she needed to do. God had worked out all the details in advance! We had a prayer and praise meeting right there in the hospital corridor!

Kamisha said she would pray for my sister and me. I asked if she would pray that Jan forgive her son who had been so kind and loving but with whom Jan, in her final illness, had become very upset through no fault of his own. I prayed she would connect with him in a merciful way before she died, and Kamisha (like a real prayer warrior) said, "What is his name? I am in a prayer group and we will be lifting your sister and her son up." I knew the power of corporate prayer and said goodbye to Kamisha with more confidence and feeling greatly comforted.

Isn't God good and all-knowing? I had two more experiences with two different women before I left that hospital that day that were clearly God appointments, even though I was trying to slip in and out quietly without upsetting Jan. The nurse at the nurse's station was extraordinarily kind and explained that this inexplicable behavior often happened after the cancer had gone to the brain. She was tender towards me as she told me that the person who caught the brunt was usually the person the patient knew could be safely taken for granted.

God orchestrated my steps to think I was going to visit Jan to minister to her; instead, He sent several people to minister to *me* tenderly and lovingly and allowed me to hear His voice. He was not leaving me nor forsaking me in my circumstances. He has always been faithful through these years. The pain from Jan's words was deep, but the joy was deeper. She did not allow me to visit with her, but she received my gifts that expressed my love for her, and that was the chief thing I wanted to express: love. We lost

Jan right after that, but she had received my gesture of love and knew I was close by in every way.

Our Abba Daddy cares for us and knows about every hurt and every worry. He is the perfect parent who never fails and is never separated from us if we call out to Him. He may send us down a "wrong" hallway if that is what He knows is needed for us to run into the blessings and provision He has in store for us.

As Luke 12:6-8 says:

Are not five sparrows sold for two pennies? Yet not one of them is forgotten by God. Indeed, the very hairs of your head are all numbered. Don't be afraid; you are worth more than many sparrows.

I tell you, whoever publicly acknowledges me before others, the Son of Man will also acknowledge before the angels of God.

Nothing happens to you that is not sifted through His hands. There are no accidents and nothing takes your Father God by surprise. Ask God to make you more aware of how He has blessed you, even though you may have felt at the time you were making a detour or wrong turn.

IV. 🐚 God Is With You in the Small "God-Touches"

Sometimes, the little love touches God gives you when you need it are the most beautiful and special moments in your relationship with Him. He may do things or show you things that are no big deal to anyone else but will be poignantly meaningful to you.

Redbirds, also called cardinals, have always been very special to me. My mother struggled with mental illness and depression, but there was something about seeing a redbird that would cheer her up. The way she would be so excited to see them made them seem like a God-touch to me. She had grown up in Georgia, but we lived in the desert of El Paso, Texas when I was young, so a redbird sighting was rare and a cause for much excitement at my house. As a child, I began to believe God would send these birds to encourage us when we most needed it.

Fast-forward thirty years. On a day of some of my darkest despair over my marriage, I was so mired down in sadness and grief that I could barely concentrate on my work in my home office. I stopped to pray, and then I walked outside to get some fresh air and feel the sun for a moment. Never before had I seen anything like this nor have I since, but on that day, my yard was covered with redbirds! There must have been 30 or 40 or more. What a beautiful sight!

I knew this was no coincidence. Only God could have known how meaningful the redbird was to me, and He had made a spectacular display of them and of His love for me that morning.

Another time, He used something not nearly as lovely to speak to me. Ezekiel 37 tells an eerie story of a vision God gave His prophet.

The hand of the LORD was upon me, and He brought me out by the Spirit of the LORD and set me down in the middle of the valley; and it was full of bones. He caused me to pass among them round about, and behold, there were very many on the surface of the valley; and lo, they were very dry. He said to me, "Son of man, can these bones live?" And I answered, "O Lord GOD, You know." Again He said to me, "Prophesy over these bones and say to them, 'O dry bones, hear the word of the LORD.' Thus says the Lord GOD to these bones, "Behold, I will cause breath to enter you that you may come to life. I will put sinews on you, make flesh grow back on you, cover you with skin and put breath in you that you may come alive; and you will know that I am the LORD."

So I prophesied as I was commanded; and as I prophesied, there was a noise, and behold, a rattling; and the bones came together, bone to its bone. And I looked, and behold, sinews were on them, and flesh grew and skin covered them; but there was no breath in them. Then He said to me, "Prophesy to the breath, prophesy, son of man, and say to the breath, 'Thus says the Lord GOD, "Come from the four winds, O breath, and breathe on these slain, that they come to life. So I prophesied as He commanded me, and the breath came into them, and they came to life and stood on their feet, an exceedingly great army.

In a two-week period in late 2014, I found this passage popping up everywhere! If I went to a class at my church, Ezekiel 37 would be one of the passages the teacher read. If I visited a friend's church, that would be the pastor's text for that day. If a friend sent me a devotional, it would be based on this Scripture. I already knew that repetitions like this are from God. I really knew it was no coincidence when one day, in traffic, I looked at the back plate on the

Mercedes in front of me and it said, "Dem Bones!" Though I knew these verses were sent to me for a purpose, I really did not know exactly what it was. Of course, God's Word is so alive and dynamic, that it can have multiple purposes and meanings simultaneously. The first purpose it had for me was to let me know that God could heal me and restore me. I have several joint problems, but the neurological damage I had experienced in childbirth had been unrelenting for 25 years. This burning, searing pain in my lower back exceeded any pain from broken bones, torn knees, or other injuries I had incurred from falling due to chronic vertigo through the years.

I had gone to many doctors, including an excellent surgeon who did a new procedure in early 2014. The treatment had worked for a couple of weeks, but when the pain came back, it was more terrible than it had been before the treatment. I was so discouraged. Another doctor told me that my pain actually never stopped, not even in my sleep, so I was tired all the time.

Months after I had given up on the doctors being able to cure me, I woke one morning and the pain was gone. I am ashamed to admit that I was in such disbelief that I did not mention it to anyone for almost a month. For me, this was too good to be true, and I was fearful it was a fluke.

Then one day, God reminded me of the Ezekiel 37 passage I had received from Him over and over. God let me know that He could "put sinews on me" and make me come alive in a way I had not been before my adult child was born. I cried when I realized what the message was.

Giving God the glory was exceptionally important. Because many people at my church had known I had gone to a new surgeon, they kept saying how great it was that the doctor had cured me. Each time, I was compelled to explain that the pain had come back with a vengeance after the doctor's procedure, and that it had stayed for five months before my sudden and supernatural healing.

So much healing comes from the hand of God and the credit is given to doctors instead. I have been grateful for the doctors who have treated me and really helped me through the years, but God uses them to facilitate healing. God still deserves the ultimate thanks and praise. Nothing good comes without His help.

It is really important to God that we are truthful and accurate about giving praise and thanks when it is due Him. It is part of our testimony. Luke 17: 11-19 tells a story that demonstrates how important it is that we give Him the thanks and the glory for our healings:

While He was on the way to Jerusalem, He was passing between Samaria and Galilee. As He entered a village, ten leprous men who stood at a distance met Him; and they raised their voices, saying, "Jesus, Master, have mercy on us!" When He saw them, He said to them, "Go and show yourselves to the priests." And as they were going, they were cleansed. Now one of them, when he saw that he had been healed, turned back, glorifying God with a loud voice, and he fell on his face at His feet, giving thanks to Him. And he was a Samaritan. Then Jesus answered and said, "Were there not ten cleansed? But the nine—where are they? Was no one found who returned to give glory to God, except this foreigner?" And He said to him, "Stand up and go; your faith has made you well."

We should purpose to be the one who stands strong to give God the praise He deserves for His mercies and touches.

This past year, God has shown me an even greater reason He kept impressing upon me the story of the resurrection of the dry bones. 2015 brought so many court decisions and legislative decisions that have been temporary but major losses for the Christians. It seemed that if a law was up for consideration that was against the teachings in the Holy Bible, then that law was passed. Looking at politics and society in this short-term view, a Christian could easily become discouraged and believe we are not on the winning side. But for 5,000 years, the prophecies in the Bible have been proven true time and time again. Christians and Jews have learned that the Bible was written with a long-term view in mind. With the longer and even eternal view of history and politics, one can have no doubt that God's will triumphs in the end. We are on the winning side, though the short term may prove to be very difficult for a while. If God can resurrect dry bones and put flesh on them and make them live again, He can resurrect our values, our society, and our very lives to be lived in a way that brings Him and us great joy.

We have pretty much let the bones of our society be stripped bare of life, goodness, and robust health, but with one Word, God can bring new life and make everything work together as it was designed to do. And one day, He will.

What in your life needs resurrection? Your marriage? Another relationship? Your neighborhood? Your faith? Your quiet time with Him? Ask Him to breathe life into whatever you feel is dead or dry right now. He has not lost His resurrection power. The power He had that allowed Him to rise from the dead is just as strong in this moment as it was back then, and you have full access to it. Take a step of faith. Ask Him to use His resurrection power on your behalf. He loves you. He will do it.

V. 🐢 God Is With You When You Must Start Over

Starting over after my divorce was a bit daunting. I had full responsibility for a mortgage, virtually nothing to my name, and a three-year-old. To make things even scarier for me, I had to make a lot of decisions very fast. My husband and I had lived next door to my in-laws, and my husband now lived with them, so I was living in our house with my son. Throughout the week, my husband would drop in unannounced and angrily chastise me for prolonged periods of time for things such as leaving the porch light on or other mistakes I made as a busy working mother. The pastor counseling me advised me that this scenario, played out over and over, was not good for my son. So even though I could scarcely face finding a new house and moving, I knew I had to do that fast. I was extremely fearful that I would make the wrong choice and hurt my son and me by putting us in the wrong neighborhood or by making a bad financial decision. As I poured out my heart to God in prayer about these fears, He gave me the peace that passes all understanding. He also did two things that helped guide me in the right direction.

After one of my evening prayer times when I asked God to guide my steps, I fell into a very deep, sweet sleep. I am one of those people who can go for years without remembering a dream, but the dream I had that night left me feeling buoyed up with joy and a feeling of well-being I can scarcely describe. In my dream, I saw a huge Palladium window through which sunlight just poured. The light filled the room, and it felt as if my soul was also being filled with God's light. Nothing happened in the dream; it was just an experience of the beauty of the window and the light.

The second thing happened as I read my Bible. Every time I picked up my Bible, God was taking me to Scriptures that said to take counsel from the men in my family—all the men. Those men were my father and my brother-in-law. I questioned God on this as my father was elderly and had not been in touch with the real estate market in years. My brother-in-law had bought a house when he was very young and had not ever moved. He is a brilliant attorney, but real estate and investments are not his forte, so I could not understand why God seemed to be telling me to listen to Him, as I had more practical knowledge of real estate than he did. Still, it was inescapable that this was God's direction.

When the realtor Cathy Meder came to take me to look at houses that first day, we looked at several acceptable choices. When she started to drive up the driveway of the last house, I said to her, "Let's call it a day. I can tell you already that I will never buy this house. I don't like the color of the brick and several other things about it. I don't want to waste your time."

My realtor was a Christian and we had prayed together at the start of this day. She was wise enough to ignore my protests and pulled right on up that driveway. Cathy said, "I want you to at least look at the craftsmanship in this house. The builder is known for having very high standards. I know you are thinking about having a house built if you don't find anything. Come in and look at the quality of this builder's work. Also, Casey, you live on the inside not the outside."

Like a balky child, I got out of the car. When we walked in, I was speechless as I saw in front of me the exact Palladium window I had seen in my dream. Sunlight filtered in through the 16-foot window and flooded the large living room. I felt tears come to my eyes as I sensed this was God's choice, even if it had not been mine. The hallways were extremely wide for a three-year-old to run down and the huge living room was perfect for an active boy. Everything was on one floor, making life easier for a busy single mom. Each feature of this house seemed designed for me, even the low maintenance yard.

As we drove out of the neighborhood, I saw on every street corner a young boy my son's age. The concentration of boys of this age in one neighborhood defied all odds, and my only child son needed playmates.

When I got home that night, I called my brother-in-law. When I told him the neighborhood, he became more excited than I ever dreamed this staid, dignified, non-emotional former judge could ever be. He enthusiastically told me that this was the neighborhood everyone in this area was predicting to be THE neighborhood, and that for resale value, I could not do better. He and my sister lived nearby, and he strongly urged me to buy the house.

My dad met me at the house the next day and instantly fell in love with the house. Without reservation, he also urged me to buy the house. After some prayer time that night when I presented all of this to the Lord, I made a decision to do just that.

I will say that I have never lived in a house that was more perfect for my needs. With each passing day, I could see how everything from the floor plan to the location seemed to be designed just for me. My son had tons of friends, and things like carpools and sharing childcare were easy for me since there were so many moms.

I entered the house buying process feeling so alone, very aware that I had no husband to advise me and to rely on. Isaiah 54:5 says, *"For your Maker is your husband-- the LORD Almighty is his name-- the Holy One of Israel is your Redeemer; he is called the God of all the earth."*

No husband could have helped me more or been a better covering of protection through this process. Is there an area where you need Him to cover you or guide you? Tell Him about it and then ask His help. And if He starts to take you down a driveway to something you think is an unattractive option, wait. Give Him a chance to show you what He is trying to show you. He may be trying to bless you. My experience tells me, "Don't fight it." As Ephesians 3:20-21 tells us:

and to know this love that surpasses knowledge—that you may be filled to the measure of all the fullness of God.

Now to him who is able to do immeasurably more than all we ask or imagine, according to his power that is at work within us, to him be glory in the church and in Christ Jesus throughout all generations, forever and ever! Amen.

His answer will be your provision even beyond what you ask or imagine. You are never alone but have the power and the presence of your God with you in every moment, even real estate closings!

VI. 🍮 God Is With You in Financial Difficulty

I never wanted to become an entrepreneur. I am the last person on earth who would have chosen this path of owning my own consulting business, but I felt God had given me no other choice.

When I married, I had a job with a large consulting firm and was about to be the first female analyst in the history of the company. My path to partnership was assured. I loved my job, but my husband did not want me to travel, so I resigned that job. All Biblical principles are designed to bless us, and I so wanted to be a Godly wife. I knew submission might be a principle I would struggle with since I had been so independent and self-sufficient, and I had loved my work. Although I suggested to my husband that we might be better off not making so many radical changes in our first year of marriage, he disagreed, so I did not hesitate to resign. In that first year, we also built a house, which necessitated moving twice from temporary residences, so my life was in chaos at home and in my career.

I began to take contracting jobs as a consultant, and this seemed to work well for me. My husband wanted me bring in a substantial income, and these contracts paid well, though there were months when there was little work and months when there was more than I could accept. No job is perfect and since I was busy dealing with the new house, this flexible schedule accommodated the many appointments I had about molding, appliances, wallpaper, and so on.

But as we experienced more and more conflict in our young marriage, my husband felt that the problem was my job. He felt I should have a more regular schedule. He believed that I would be better suited to a 9 to 5 job, and he suggested a job in a traditional environment such as a bank. Finding a banking job that paid the income he desired I earn was difficult, as I was not a finance major. I finally found a job as an organizational development consultant and sales trainer with First National Bank of Atlanta, later to merge with Wachovia. I had many adjustments to make, but I settled in and had begun to enjoy the job and to love my co-workers. At about that time, my husband and I were arguing almost daily. One of the problems was that I was not free to do all the things his friends' wives did who were not working outside the home. Making myself available to travel with him on golf trips and other events seemed to be a good idea so that we could experience some good times together and not just the bad times we were having now. We decided I needed to resign this job as well.

I must give you a bit of background so you will know some of the inner conflict I was experiencing as I made these first year adjustments. I am not a job hopper. I kept my first job with Rich's Department Store all through high school, college, and a bit longer after I graduated. I had quit my consulting contracting job in less than a year and now I was about to quit another job. Still, I felt that if leaving Wachovia might help my marriage in any way, I should be willing to try, so I began to look for another job that met the required salary yet that would allow me to travel.

As I thought about it, I realized that owning my own consulting practice rather than working for someone else would allow me more freedom in creating my own schedule. The only thing that kept me from it was that the thought of running a business by myself was daunting, and I really didn't know how I would bring in new clients. Still, my husband thought this was a great idea, so I started my own consulting practice.

Women who resist the Godly version of submission miss out on some unbelievable blessings. When we yield our will to His, He does amazing things in our lives.

Before I ever resigned, God brought me a steady client that would cover my basic expenses and pay me a decent base all year long, so He immediately took one of my fears away—the fear of losing money. Although some travel was involved, at this point my husband actually wanted me to be away some, since things were very difficult between us. So I resigned with a cushion.

On my first week on the job, I had planned to write a business plan and create my marketing materials. I had been a consultant to businesses for years and knew this was the correct way to start. I have now been in business for over 25 years and have never created that business plan nor even a professional brochure. In the very competitive world of communication consulting, God has brought to my doorstep all the business I have needed every step of the way.

On the very first day in my tiny home office as I started my business, my phone rang. It was a human resource manager in charge of training for Equifax. She had a need for a consultant on business writing, and someone gave her my name. She asked that I come down the next day as she needed to move fast. I wanted to say, "Wait! I need to get my brochure created and printed first," but I knew not to hesitate when an actual project was practically offered to me over the phone.

I put together a one-page list of the courses I might offer, and that one-page 81/2 by 11 sheet has been the closest thing I have had for a brochure for over twenty-five years. Not only did I do a great deal of work for Equifax, later they would want to take my writing course worldwide. Since I could not cover all the international locations, they paid me royalties for my course and taught it themselves! I had never dreamed I could have passive income without lifting a finger! God blessed me "immeasurably more than all we ask or imagine, according to his power." Ephesians 3:20

The day I went to meet with Equifax, a friend said to me, "Don't waste the pretty." I said, "What do you mean?" She said, "If you have to put on pantyhose and a suit, take that one-page list of what you do to another company or two." I did that and that created more business.

At some point during that first year of business, another friend suggested I go talk to her husband who was a training manager at Bellsouth. I went to talk to him about doing my own courses, but instead, he wanted me to do some video-based courses for him. Because I did not own the material and because I would just be facilitating the video lessons, the pay was a fraction of what I would normally receive. I started to graciously but firmly say "no," but at that moment I got a strong urging in my heart to say "yes." I wasn't entirely obedient, but I did ask for some time to think it over. After going home and praying about it, I sensed strongly there was an inexplicable reason for me to accept this low paying job. I thought perhaps there was a divine appointment for me to introduce someone there to the Lord or that the job would lead to better things. I would never have guessed the real reason God told me to accept a video-based program.

By the time I showed up to conduct my first video-based class, I was pregnant. By the third month, I was having complications and the doctor wanted me to stay off my feet. The programs I had always done before had required me to be on my feet for up to seven hours a day. The video-based program would have me on my feet for 15 to 30 minutes at time, and then I would sit for an hour while the tape taught the class. In the middle of the day, there was a two-hour team assignment. Each team of students would create a project in their respective breakout rooms with no instructor involvement. I could take a two-hour lunch break each day and eat at a lovely salad place down the street. This arrangement was probably more relaxing than staying home, and it met my doctors' requirements for staying off my feet for long periods of time. If I had scheduled more of my own courses, I would have had to cancel most of them and would have had almost no income during my pregnancy. Though the pay was low on the video courses, I had steady income until my ninth month when I was forced to stop doing the seminar work.

While I was working at half-speed, another friend called me who was bidding on some work for Georgia Power, a great company that was practically right in my back yard. She was bidding on some presentation courses for the company, but the company wanted a vendor who also had a strong proposal-writing course. She asked if she could present me as their associate who would do the writing courses through my company. I agreed and wrote a proposal that the manager of industrial marketing loved. We met in November, and he wanted to do the pilot in mid-December. The problem was that my baby was due

December 24, so I asked that the pilot be delayed until February 24. The new date would give me eight weeks at home with my baby and to regain my strength. This highly regarded gentleman and powerful decision-maker agreed to my request.

My son always did things on his own terms. He waited as long as possible to be born. I was scheduled to be induced into labor on January 24, but I went into natural labor instead. Still, this little guy was four weeks late, giving me only four weeks to get strong after an unusually hard birthing experience.

During those four weeks, the only money we had was what was in my purse. I had stockpiled all the formula and diapers the baby would need, but cash was in short supply. I had saved $4000 to tide us over for the eight weeks I couldn't work. My hospital bill had been astronomical due to my complications that required me to stay in the hospital for a full week. We could never have anticipated that all the care I needed during my delivery would have resulted in the hospital presenting us with a bill for the entire $4000 for our part! I left the hospital with no money. My husband had shared with me that he had not been able to earn money in his real estate business for a couple of years, so he had even less. The video program at Bellsouth had ended in November, so I had nothing on the horizon for 1989 except the one pilot course for Georgia Power, to be delivered on my baby's four-week birthday.

I was still pretty weak when I went to present my pilot course to them. The room was full of marketing people who had successfully written proposals for years and who were not very excited about taking a writing course. They had been asked to be very critical as the decision to hire a vendor would mean an investment. I was lightheaded often through that first day, and I wasn't sure how coherent my answers were to their questions.

God often works this way to bless me. The greatest financial blessings of my life have been given to me in such a way that I had no doubt they were from the hand of God. There is no way I could look at that day of the pilot course and think, "My performance was what won the business" or "What quick-witted answers I gave to their questions." God took what I put out there, pitiful as it was, and transformed it into a course that would be offered at Georgia Power for over 20 years, with ongoing updates! Within a week of the pilot, people were calling me from all over that company to book the course. I booked $52,000 in business that first year, and my business grew with them. Georgia Power allowed me to work close to home and with a very family friendly company that cared about their employees and even their vendors. I will always be grateful to George Haynes, the manager who took a chance on me and waited till my son was born so I could do that pilot. He and his wife Linda and their beloved son Justin are still in my life as people I care about very much.

God had again given me exactly what I needed, a steady client that gave me a high volume of business. Usually, a consultant is constantly rewriting and readapting material for new clients. I could barely keep up with the business at Georgia Power in the first few years of my son's life. But I was doing duplicates of the same course over and over again, so my preparation time was greatly reduced. When I ended my seminars at 3:00, their preferred stop time, I was free to enjoy my son. I could only do one seminar a week, so that meant that I was at Georgia Power two short days a week and free the rest of the week to be a full-time mom.

But life began to grow more complicated at work and at home. Things began to get frighteningly worse between my husband and me. I had tried to support him in his dream of starting his own business as a real estate broker, but business was not good in those years and he was miserable.

The fighting at our house would last late into the night. Georgia Power was asking that I conduct a seminar at their Savannah office, even though I had a no-travel policy when my baby was so young. I was feeling I was away from my baby more than I wanted to be and that with the stress in our house, I assumed (without praying) that God wanted me to stay home more with my son. And though I was content with my earnings, my husband was disappointed that I was not making more money; I was to learn later why he felt this way. He told me it was because we did not have the money to travel as much as he would like and that we did not have the money to join a second golf club he very much wanted to join.

Then one day, everything converged to give me almost more than I could bear. By this time, my husband and I were in the process of divorcing. I was reluctantly about to leave on a trip to Savannah to teach that writing course when my husband broke the news to me about the staggering debt he had incurred for us. In those days he gambled, and as a result, he had accumulated thousands of dollars of debt I had been unaware of. He told me he had not been able to earn money to cover the debt because of a slow real estate market. Then an attorney explained that if I were the only one with a real and stable income, that the banks would expect me to pay all the debts. Pursuing my husband would yield them nothing.

As a single woman, I had never let a credit card go for over a month. I was brought up to avoid debt. And now I was about to be a single mom with a toddler and a mountain of crushing debt on my shoulders alone. I could have sold the house to pay off the debt, but I very much wanted to stay in a house for my son's sake rather than in an apartment, even though the house came with a mortgage. I wanted the stability of a neighborhood of families and role models from two-parent homes.

I arrived in Savannah late that night, went into my hotel room, and cried out to God. I told Him that I knew He said He does not give us more than we can bear, and I told Him that I could not bear this. It was too much. I also told Him that I knew He had been telling me to cut back on work to be a better mom, but how could I do that and handle these debts? At one point, I cried out to Him, "I would have to double my rates if I were to stay home more and pay off these debts!" And that was ridiculous, I thought. I was already being paid a good rate. Consultants don't just double their rates. That was crazy. But when I cried it out, I felt this peace come over me that said, "But that is the solution." I fought against the idea for days. Still, it was the time of year when consultants were proposing courses and prices for the next year. Could the timing be far from coincidental?

I felt very sure I was being urged to step out on faith and double my rates. I am in a field that has lower than average consulting fees. Many English, communications and marketing professors do similar workshops to mine as sidelines to their teaching and are willing to work for very low fees. How could I possibly ask for such a substantial raise?

In my own strength, I could have never negotiated such a rate increase. But when God is telling you, "Here is the solution to your problem," it is much easier to stay strong.

I doubled my fees and barely heard a ripple of complaint. I lost no customers. Only God could have given me this surprising and generous result. God is the best business partner I could have ever had.

The final example of God's faithfulness to me in some very difficult circumstances came five years later in 1996. After having plenty of business for the first seven years of my little company, my business suddenly dried up. What happened? The Olympics happened.

Though I am so happy that my son and I got to enjoy the thrill of the Olympics, it was a perfect storm for me where my business was concerned. At that time, my most active clients were Bellsouth, Georgia Power, and Georgia Pacific. These three companies were the most involved in building the equivalent of a new city within Atlanta that would become venues and services for the Olympics. All other activity in the city ground to a halt. No one really thought Atlanta would land the Olympics, so no one was prepared financially or otherwise. Business was impacted, not just for the duration of the Olympics, but also for the intense six months prior to the games as construction and meetings and planning took place.

I lost business for three reasons. First, panicky meetings were taking place in local Atlanta companies where executives were being asked to give up money from their budgets to build and manage the venues; the easiest place to cut was training and consulting. It's a lot less painful to cut consultants than employees. Almost all workshops were canceled. Second, my clients were decision-makers and were asked to carve out extra time to think through the logistics of telecommunications, electricity and construction required by this massive project. They simply did not have the time to work on strategic plans and other complex documents that I normally helped them develop. Finally, meeting space is limited in downtown Atlanta. At that time, it was not unusual for companies to rent hotel meeting space for my classes. All hotel space had been booked months in advance as soon as the announcement was made that Atlanta would host. The space was used for planning meetings by the media, the Olympic staff, and others who would sponsor and support the Olympics. Writing workshops fell to the bottom of the list of priorities.

Of course, at the time I didn't realize what was happening. The impact of the Olympics on small business was something most Atlantans were unaware of. All I knew was that my phone stopped ringing except for cancellations. It was discouraging and bewildering.

As I began to hear my clients' reasons for canceling, it began to be apparent that the Olympic planning was at the root of the problem. If that were so, I did not want to give up a business that had provided such a good schedule and a good income for my son and me. Although I was not sure, I felt that if I could weather the next six months that my business would come back. I prayed and asked God if He wanted me to take a 9 to 5 job to pay the bills, but I did not feel His urging to do that. I explored contracting situations but nothing was available short term in my area. As the months progressed, my funds were running dangerously low. My confidence ebbed. I had been on the

Internet for days looking for work. I had written to companies who were looking for full-time writers, asking if they would allow me to do the work on a contract basis until they hired someone. No one had responded.

Late one night as I scoured the local job ads on AJC.com, I became completely discouraged. I cried out to God. I said, "I am fighting as hard as I can not to be discouraged and not to live in fear, but my circumstances are bad. I have a young child, a mortgage, old debts I am still paying, and my rainy day money is almost gone. I am not going to give in to it though, because You tell us not to look at our circumstances but to look to you. So I am looking to You right now. "

I sat at my computer sobbing these words to the Lord at midnight, all by myself as my child slept at the end of the hall.

I said, "Lord, I am going to say out loud all the things I know to be true because satan is whispering lies to me. If I don't drown him out with the truth, I will be tempted to despair and believe his lies. Here are some things that I know are true: I know you are a good God. I know you have promised to never leave me nor forsake me. I know that all things are supposed to work to bless me, but Lord, how can this possibly be a blessing? I am not doubting You for a minute, but please show me how this is a blessing! I need your encouragement to make it through this."

And then I felt a real calm and sense of well-being come over me. I knew His Holy Spirit had filled my heart and taken the place of the despair that had threatened to take me over. Once that happened, I was able to think clearly for the first time in the recent stress-filled weeks. I began to think very logically and this scripture came to my mind:

Delight thyself also in the LORD, and He shall give thee the desires of thine heart. Psalm 37:4

I thought, "Okay, what is the desire of your heart?" I had my wonderful son that was such a gift, but I felt the Lord was saying, "What is something you have always dreamed of and wanted?" And I knew what it was immediately. Since I was in the third grade, I had wanted to write a book. And with His very personal sense of humor, I felt God saying, "What is stopping you? You certainly have nothing else to do. You have tried to get jobs and nothing is happening. I have cleared your calendar for you because you did not have the courage to do it yourself. You might as well write that book!"

And I did. When you are inspired, the words just pour out of you. I wrote my first book in just a few weeks. Experienced writers had long ago told me all the tricks of the trade, but I did nothing the way I should have. They told me to submit the book to a dozen publishers, but I only submitted it to one, the one I wanted most of all. They told me not to bother sending it because no reputable publisher would even open the envelope if I did not have an agent. But I dropped the proposal and the manuscript into a brown envelope and sent it to the publisher I most wanted to publish it, and told my friends I would do it their way if it did not work out. My manuscript miraculously caught the eye of Grace Freedson, senior editor at Barron's Educational, and she became my advocate there. To make a long story short, I wrote my first three books for them. Later, Grace left to be an agent. She asked me to be one of her first clients. I have now published with McGraw-Hill and Ten-speed, an imprint of Random House.

Only God could take my failures and inexperience and turn them into a career that is the desire of my heart. Only God can take the ashes of our lives and turn them into joy.

Some family members believe this all happened because I have tithed since I was nine years old. Even when I did not know Him personally, I remembered this rule and for some reason followed it for most of my life. I disagree. I don't think God did this because I am good but because *He* is good and loves His children.

Which of you, if your son asks for bread, will give him a stone? Or if he asks for a fish, will give him a snake?
Matthew 7:9-10

He is your father who loves you so much He would do anything for you if it is in your best interest. No price is too high to pay for your freedom and peace and joy. He even sacrificed His beloved Son, His only perfect child Jesus, to pay a ransom for you. Do you think He is unwilling to answer your prayers? No. Just as it delights us as parents to gift our children with wonderful things and to provide for their needs, He is even more that way.

Don't hesitate to have a talk with Him today about the desires of your heart. Just as we parents love to have our children tell us of their love for us, God loves to hear these words, too. If you have never trusted Him this way, tell Him you want to trust Him. Ask Him to reveal Himself to you. Ask Him for His help to trust Him fully. Then give Him time and give Him an open mind to show you He loves you. It may not be overnight, but He will not let you down if you truly seek Him with your whole heart.

The final example of God's goodness to me is more recent. After that difficult time in 1996 and for the next 17 years, my business was financially strong. My book royalties and speaking fees amply provided for all our needs. Then in

July of 2013, Belinda Stone, my dear friend and the beloved director of Women's Ministry at our church died of cancer. The church asked two of my friends and me to serve as leaders until a new director could be hired. Although I attend a very large church and this would be a demanding job, I accepted, thinking it would only be a matter of weeks until a new director would be hired. Instead, the task took over a year. The needs were mammoth and the widespread grief over losing Belinda created even more demands for me to be at church and comfort the women. We were doing everything for the first time: deciding what Bible Studies to do for the following year, choosing speakers for big events, figuring out budget and invoicing processes, and a hundred other things. As I poured my life more and more into the church, I completely neglected my consulting business. I was earning enough income from the business that had already been planned prior to July, but I had no time to visit clients about new projects, and I was so busy I was referring out more and more business to other consultants because I simply did not have the time. I did not even realize how I was painting myself into a financial corner by not providing work for myself in the coming year. As 2013 drew to an end, I looked around and realized I was about to have a precipitous drop in income starting in January of 2014. I also had not remembered to pay quarterly taxes and had a huge tax bill to pay in 2014 as well as some upcoming medical expenses that could not be postponed. There was no work on the horizon for me, and my clients needed nothing at that time. I was in a full-blown panic the day I realized the dire situation I was in. I prayed quietly, but to be honest, I was physically weak from the realization of my predicament, so I resolved to pray more earnestly the next morning when I was fresh.

The next morning I remembered a book someone had once given me by Bill Gothard, *The Power of Crying Out.* This book is based on Psalm 18:6:

In my distress I called to the LORD; I cried to my God for help. From his temple he heard my voice; my cry came before him, into his ears.

A Bible study teacher had once taught me that the verb "cry" in this verse meant literally to cry loudly. I had nothing to lose and was desperate and felt I was supposed to do this.

I felt sheepish, but I stood in the middle of my bedroom and cried out to the Lord in my distress all about my problem and told Him my every need. I was even very specific about the exact sum I needed to pay taxes, bills, and give me a comfortable margin for the first half of 2014. As I prayed at the top of my voice, I felt less sheepish by the minute and felt stronger and stronger. At the end of that prayer time, all feelings of panic had gone.

What happened next made no earthly sense. I had told my agent Grace a couple of years before to stop calling me with offers for me to write business books. I had not felt led to sign on for a long-term writing commitment for a couple of years. I thought writing for business was a thing of the past for me. And Grace also knew that I would not look at any project that did not pay royalties. I had been consistent in always foregoing a larger upfront fee for the prospect of long-term royalties. So I was shocked and even a little offended when I got up off my knees from prayer, and the phone rang with Grace's offer. She was offering me a book project and there were no royalties, just an upfront sum. At first, I brushed the offer off and was a bit disappointed in the normally very astute Grace for not realizing this offer did not fit my parameters or that I did not even want a book project at all. I hung up, took two steps away from the phone, and it hit me. The upfront sum offered was the exact sum I had told the Lord I needed!

For the second time that morning, I went to my knees and prayed—this time for forgiveness for my vast and overwhelming pride that had blinded me to God's immediate provision for all my needs. I was repulsed and ashamed by the ugliness of my attitude and the arrogance of my heart. I got off my knees the second time with a heart full of gratitude and went into my home office to call Grace to say I would be glad to accept the offer.

Is God trying to answer one of your prayers in a way that you cannot recognize or appreciate? Do you have one way you want your prayer to be answered and are you rejecting another door God is opening for you?

Examine your heart. Then ask God to reveal to you any pride issues you may have or any way you have blocked hearing His will. Ask Him to open the eyes of your heart so you can see, as described in Ephesians 1:18-19:

I pray that the eyes of your heart may be enlightened, so that you will know what is the hope of His calling, what are the riches of the glory of His inheritance in the saints, and what is the surpassing greatness of His power toward us who believe.NASB

Give God time to answer your prayer through reading His Word, by hearing the preaching of His Word, and through Godly counselors. This approach can lead to your own adventure in Christianity.

VII. ❧ God Is With You in Death

Three times in my life have I been near death. In each case, God revealed Himself to me in the most incredible ways, and these experiences have left me unafraid of death and more aware of the gift of life. Before these experiences, I was so afraid of death. I was not afraid of what happened after death as I knew I was saved, and I knew exactly what would happen the moment my death experience was over; however, walking through the actual experience of death was terrifying to me. The Lord showed me that He would walk through everything with me, even this final moment on earth, and never leave my side. Here is how He gently taught me of His constancy and that I could count on Him in ALL things.

My work as a consultant and speaker on business communication often took me to locations all over the United States. I flew so often that turbulent weather or bumpy air did not faze me. All experienced travelers know that happens often, but most of us don't think much about the infrequent crashes unless the media makes a crash a lead story.

Just such a dramatic crash happened before a return trip I was making from Florida. Every magazine and television news program ran footage of a little girl who had survived a terrible crash where almost everyone had been killed. Her survival was attributed to her mother who had strapped her body over the little girl's in her seat, and had taken the brunt of the fiery crash for her. By all accounts, the little girl was fine. At the time, I paid this story little mind.

As I boarded the plane, I noticed that almost all the passengers looked as if they were business travelers, a bit bored and blasé with the entire experience of flying. These world-weary road warriors were fastidiously dressed and sophisticated. They collectively looked cool, confident, and used to being in control.

We heard the engines start up as usual, felt ourselves taxiing down the runway, and then felt the usual lift-off from the ground into the air. A few seconds later, we knew something was terribly wrong. One side of the plane kept dipping wildly and the plane was tipping to the left, and then it would level and then it would immediately start its wild dipping again. It was terrifying. Then I remembered that at the end of the runway was water, and I began to wonder if our next dip would take us into the ocean and to the end of our lives. The pilot, who was doing an incredible job of keeping us aloft, came on the speaker to prepare us. He told us that we had lost our nose-wheel steering, some or all of the hydraulic system, and possibly other functions as well. He said we needed to return immediately to the airport we had just left, but that naturally, we would have to dump as much of the fuel from the very full tanks as we could before we landed. I don't think any sight has ever been as somber to me as when I looked out my window and saw hundreds of gallons of jet fuel streaming out of the plane. This was not a drill; we were preparing for what seemed to be an inevitable crash. I felt sad that I probably was never going to see my husband, my family, and my friends again, but I felt a peace I could not explain. I have never been more sure of my faith and where my final destination would be if I did not survive the plane crash. I can tell you now that God is there in life and death moments. He supplies that comfort when you need it, and not before. The Bible says He gives us the peace that passes all understanding, and I experienced that inexplicable peace that day. The circumstances were terrifying, but I was not afraid of the future.

Peace and calm were not what I saw all around me. Flight attendants were trying to soothe hysterical people and you could hear people quietly crying all over the cabin. Some were angry. Gone were the blasé expressions and confident looks of the sophisticated road warriors. We were very likely about to experience death, and most faces looked ashen with fear.

Then I saw one of the most beautiful acts of love I have ever witnessed.

I wanted to look around and see the people throughout the cabin. I wanted to take it all in during what might be my last minutes of life. I saw a mother peering into her young daughter's face, talking intently to the child who appeared to be about four or five. There was so much love on the mother's face in that moment that I cannot describe it to you. Her face was gentle and relaxed, communicating calm and love with each word she said. I had to hear what she was saying, so I strained to pay closer attention to her words.

She said, "I love you so much. Do you know I love you? No matter what happens, I want you to promise me that you know I love you. And even if something happens, I will love you forever. Nothing that may happen today is your fault. I just love you with all my heart. Now I am going to do something that may be uncomfortable, but I promise it is the best thing, and I am sorry if it hurts a bit. You know I love you, my sweet girl."

Then the mother elevated her body over her daughter's and strapped herself in over the girl as we made our final descent. In that moment, I realized the mother was doing exactly what the mother of the girl who had survived the plane crash had done, and with this act, was probably sacrificing her life for her child's. In this moment of impending death, God showed me beauty and love and courage.

The pilot had told us that since the other hydraulics were not working, that our brakes probably would not either, but miraculously they did. It was a rough landing, but no one was harmed and we were able to walk off the plane, shaken but untouched.

I will never forget the look of complete love on that mother's face that day or her bravery. But the picture of love and sacrifice taught me something else. I realized I had seen a picture of the kind of love Jesus has for me. He did not have to, but out of a deep tenderness in His heart toward me, He sacrificed His life so that I could live. He loves you the same way. Even if you were the only person on earth, He would have willingly allowed His death in order to give you life—even life after death. It is your miracle, too.

In the book of John, Chapter 10, verses 17-18, Jesus tells us:

Therefore My Father loves Me, because I lay down My life that I may take it again. No one takes it from Me, but I lay it down of Myself. I have power to lay it down, and I have power to take it again. This command I have received from My Father.

Your Heavenly Father loves you more tenderly than anyone on earth has ever loved you. He was willing to make the greatest sacrifice just for you.

You would think that after that experience, I would have avoided air travel but I continued to fly, even after I became pregnant. Money was tight, and I was conducting management seminars all over the United States on interpersonal and written communication. One of my favorite clients was Duquesne Power. I left my home in Atlanta one sunny day and boarded a flight to Pittsburgh to speak to a group of their customer service employees the next day. When we got about one hundred miles from Pittsburgh, the pilot's voice came over the speaker to make an announcement. He was genuinely relaxed and unconcerned as he said, "We have an unusual weather situation at this time. I know you Atlanta people are used to tornadoes, but they are not as common in the Pittsburgh area; however, there is tornado-like activity here today. This is no problem because we have an abundance of fuel and can wait till this weather passes through. When the high winds end, we will then be able to land with no problem, but there will be a delay. We have enough fuel to stay up here waiting for almost an extra hour, and the way winds like this move, we should not need nearly that much time."

We passengers felt comforted as we could tell that the pilot was very calm and even seemed to find the unusual weather interesting. We were assured that the winds would move on quickly and that we could land. But they did not. The tornado producing conditions stubbornly stayed in the area we would need to pass through to land. We were at 40,000 feet, the circular winds were below us, and Pittsburgh was below the winds. As the fuel dwindled, the pilot came back on the speaker and said, "Although there is still wind, because we are running low on fuel, we will need to go ahead and land. Be prepared for a rough descent and landing." This time, the pilot did not sound relaxed, and we could sense that he was very concerned.

The flight attendants prepared us by reviewing the position for us to take for a rough landing and by showing us how to use the oxygen masks, just in case they were needed—and soon they were. About the time we started the descent, we seemed to be thrust strongly to the left, and then all the oxygen went out of the cabin. The plane was banged around in the air and tossed about like a tin can. For the first time in my life, I was cut off from a supply of oxygen. All my life, I had taken for granted that next breath and the oxygen God gave me to breathe. Only in the complete absence of oxygen in that plane did I finally understand that each breath is a gift from God, and it seemed I would never again feel that precious, life-giving air fill my lungs again. The oxygen masks dropped, but we were alarmed to find that they were not functioning. We could get no air from the useless masks that hung from the ceiling. As the seconds went on and on, I knew these were probably my last moments of consciousness and life on this earth. I felt so guilty because I was depriving my unborn child of oxygen. I could bear losing my life, but my maternal instincts had kicked in, and I felt I had not protected my baby who was probably going to die without ever drawing that first sweet breath. I was ashamed for continuing to travel and for accepting this engagement, no matter how desperately we needed the money. But then God gave me a feeling of comfort and peace I cannot describe. I felt His love and forgiveness and a real closeness to Him in that moment. I was so lightheaded and felt I was blacking out when suddenly the life-giving oxygen began to flow through the mask on my face. Never again would I take the next breath for granted. God is the giver of every good gift, and no gift is a small gift, even if we don't take the time to realize it.

After the flight, I was found to be in perfect health as was my baby. God had protected that tiny life that had needed the oxygen as much as I had.

I was particularly protective of my baby because I had had to fight for his life already in the earliest months of my pregnancy. This next life or death story is not mine, but my child's.

I was a thirty-eight year old mother, so the obstetrician was keeping a close eye on me. After some routine tests, he asked to talk to my husband and me in his office. He had never done this before, so I knew it was serious. He informed us that my body was unable to give the baby the protein he needed to develop. Babies like this can suffer all kinds of damage, particularly brain damage. Though my doctor was pro-life, he said it was his duty to tell us that he did not think I could carry my precious baby full term or that even if I did that there would likely be problems, and we needed to prepare ourselves. My husband asked if terminating the pregnancy were an option. My doctor admitted it was, but he would not perform such a procedure. I now know it was because of his Christian beliefs.

When we left the doctor's office, my husband and I had a long talk. My husband said he was not prepared to raise a brain-damaged or disabled child. He felt it would be a terrible thing for our marriage and for him personally. I tried to be as sympathetic as I could, but I had to say that I knew I would not have an abortion. With great shame, I confess I had had an abortion previously in the first weeks of an earlier pregnancy when my bleeding had been nonstop because of an IUD that was still implanted when I became pregnant. Though I was assured that that almost imperceptible baby had already been dead before that procedure, it had haunted me, and I knew I had made a terrible mistake. This baby was very real to me, and I was not going to make that life or death decision again. I knew now, even more than then, that life was only for God to give and take. Like most women with my regrettable experience, I would never do that again now that I knew how precious that life was that was taken.

I promised my husband that I would never ask him for help to care for or to support this baby if he turned out to be damaged in some way, but that I could not agree to terminate the pregnancy.

In those days, I was almost a vegetarian, with the exception of some chicken or fish occasionally. All that changed from that day on. I began to eat red meat every day. If my clients took me to a restaurant, I would order steak instead of the green salad they were used to seeing me order. I did everything in my power to give my baby all the protein I could ingest!

My precious son was born at a whopping 9 pounds, defying all the predictions! If anyone had had any doubts about the condition of my child's brain, he put those to rest with perfect APGAR scores. Six months later, when I had taken him with me to my appointment with my neurologist, the doctor asked me if he could test my baby's mental acuity. The neurologist, Dr. Re, said, "In my volunteer work, I test babies whom DFACS suspects have been neglected and abused and perhaps brain damaged. Many of them have fetal alcohol syndrome. I rarely get to test a child who is on the high end of the spectrum, and I think your baby may be. May I test him?

After the test, Dr. Re was amazed and amused. He said, "I have never seen a baby do what your child just did. He passed all the tests with flying colors. The final test was a series of motions I did and then evaluated how he reacted. He did them perfectly for a while, but then he became bored and began doing the motions and testing me! He is extremely intelligent."

I believe God gave my son the gift of the intellect he has, in part, to say to women who are considering abortions, "Don't believe everything that the doctors and the world are telling you. God can defy all odds. God can make a way. God can make a baby who is predicted to be a burden be the best gift of your life." I also know this was God's affirmation of my trusting Him to care for my precious baby and for me. He has been faithful time and time again, and He has never failed us.

In each of these experiences of life and death, God showed up. God does not do tricks or reveal Himself the way we design. But if you are willing to accept Him as Lord of your life, He will never fail to be there for you. He will be all you need, but you first have to take that leap of faith and say, "God, I am accepting that you are the one true God. I am willing to trust you and believe in you."

In Mark 9, we learn the story of a father who is anguished over his son who has terrible convulsions. He takes the boy to Jesus and asks Him to heal the child.

The father says, *"But if you can do anything, take pity on us and help us."*

"'If you can'?" said Jesus. "Everything is possible for one who believes."

Immediately the boy's father exclaimed, "I do believe; help me overcome my unbelief!"

You may be wishing you could believe so you could have a Father like God. Ask Him to help you overcome your unbelief, and then give Him a chance. Wait on the Lord. He is already there waiting on you. He has been waiting on you a long time.

VIII. ❧ God Is With You When Your Health Fails

I was blessed with robust health for most of my life. Although my sister was frail and sickly, fighting pneumonia, allergies, and even a collapsed lung when we were children, I was consistently healthy and had an unusually high energy level. When you are healthy, you take it for granted like taking the sun coming up in the morning for granted. I might say in a passing prayer, "Thank you for my health," but I did not feel the deep sense of gratitude for it that I feel today, after a time when my health was taken away for a season.

Several factors combined to make my transformation from a remarkably healthy person to a near invalid. I had a complete reversal in my health. I had always had hypothyroidism, a condition that leads to weight gain and a host of other symptoms, including low blood pressure. Through diet and a medication that is excellent for that condition, I was able to ward off these symptoms and lead a normal life. When I was thirty-eight, however, I came off the medication because my thyroid system was behaving erratically. One month I would produce almost none of the hormones my body needed, and the next month I would produce a normal amount for the first time in twenty years! The problem was that when I produced the normal amount and then added the medication supplement on top of that, I would become sick. I decided to come off the medication entirely for a while to see what my body was doing. It was in this time that I became pregnant.

Although because of my age, my delivery was considered high risk, I was unconcerned. I had always been blessed with unusual strength. I remember buying a huge air conditioner second hand one time, and proudly lifting it into my car by myself. I worked right up to the day of the delivery, not realizing that I needed the rest it would take me to deliver my son. Because of some difficulties at home, I had been up till the wee hours several mornings, so I entered into labor exhausted. Despite my weariness, I still felt that labor would not be that hard. Didn't thousands of women do it every day?

I was so excited that I would finally see my son that I joyfully called my sister Bobbi when my water broke and the doctor said it was time to go to the hospital. I remember laughing when my sister beat me to the hospital. The admitting nurse said, "You won't be laughing in a little while." We did not know then how right she was.

I postponed it as long as I could, but after several hours, I requested the epidural my doctor had arranged for. As I had been instructed to do, I carefully explained to the anesthesiologist that I had low blood pressure, even though that information was prominently written on all my admission papers. The anesthesiologist administered the correct dosage and all was well.

The first problem was that I was in the pushing phase for far too long. To complicate things further, during the first 20 hours of my labor, several anesthesiologists had gone on and off duty. Somewhere along the way, as I entered the final time of labor, an anesthesiologist did not notice the warning on my chart and my blood pressure bottomed out. My mother told me later she thought she had witnessed my death.

Here is what I remember from that experience. Before the nurses or monitoring equipment picked up on anything, I felt my life ebbing from my body. I looked at my mother and said, "Mother, pray for me. I am dying."

Then I heard all kinds of alarms go off on the monitoring equipment. Someone called a code on me. I knew it was serious when I saw the nurses physically shoving my mother and husband out of the room.

I had time to pray for my baby before I lost consciousness. I was not afraid. I felt an inexplicable comfort that I know was God. Though I did not know much about God at that point, I felt His presence, and that one way or another, all would be well. I did not know if that meant all would be well in Heaven or on this earth, but I was comforted. God says we will be comforted, and in that moment, though I was not walking closely with Him, I was comforted. I was spared not because I was a good Christian, because, believe me, I was not; I was spared because He is good, and He had a purpose for me still.

I lost all respiration, and though I did not follow up to confirm it, someone told me my heart stopped. People ask me if I walked toward the light. It was not that clear. It was just a feeling of light versus dark, the sweetest, most comforting presence imaginable. In the midst of a situation that should have been full of fear and panic, I experienced complete calm.

I was aware of how hard the nurses and doctors were working to revive me, but I was still not conscious. The moment I did regain consciousness, a nurse hovered over my face and said, "I can bring you back. You are not going to die. Whatever happens, don't worry because I can bring you back. You are going to be okay, but don't give up."

I remember thanking her to encourage her and because my heart had gone out to her as she gave her all to revive me; but I knew for sure, she had not brought me back. God had. I don't know how I knew this as I was pretty ignorant about God and His ways at that time, but somehow He had met me in that experience and had made Himself known to me.

I was in the hospital for five days recovering from that horrific delivery. Nursing students had been brought in to witness the last hour of the delivery to see what could happen when things go wrong. The doctor was furious they were admitted, but I heard someone tell the students it was the bloodiest delivery they had ever seen. Apparently, some internal bleeding had built up, and at some point broke free and flooded the room. But despite it all, my blood pressure bottoming out, the chaos in the delivery room, the problem with anesthesia, I was safe, my baby was perfectly healthy, and we were both so happy.

I was, however, very weak when I left the hospital, and I had a nagging backache. People told me that I had had back labor, and that, of course, I should expect some back pain. I felt this was unusually bad pain, but I waited. My primary motivation for waiting was that I was enjoying my baby so much, and I did not want to spend one minute away at any appointments. I did have to return to work right away, since I was self-employed, but every minute possible, I was with him.

When the pain had not gone away in three months, and had, in fact, worsened, I no longer could endure it. I had to see a doctor. I consulted my sister Bobbi, the nurse in the family who always guides us to the best doctors. As usual, she rightly discerned that this was neurological rather than orthopedic. She recommended Dr. Peter Re, a legendary neurologist in our community. An ex-military man, he was known for not mincing words and for his brilliant intellect. When I found out that I would have to wait two more months to get an appointment with him, I agreed despite my pain. I wanted the best.

When I went to see him, the appointment was uneventful. He took x-rays, did some tests, and asked some questions. He seemed pretty "business as usual" and gave me exercises to do to alleviate the pain. That was at 3:00PM.

At 8:00PM, I received a panicked call from Dr. Re—not his nurse, but the man himself. "Do not do those exercises," he said firmly. "Be at the hospital at 8:00am tomorrow. You have done serious damage to your back. In fact, based on your x-rays, I don't see how you walked in here like that."

I was there early and prepared for the first of many procedures on my back. At some point later, a surgeon Dr. Re had recommended sat with my husband and me to talk to us about my condition.

As we sat in that office, the surgeon turned to my husband and said, "You need to begin to prepare yourself for her to be disabled. Her condition will not get better. Her condition will deteriorate with time. She will need help, lots of help, particularly because you have a baby. She can't possibly do all the lifting and bending a new baby requires."

My husband looked at him in disbelief and said, "Disabled? As in a wheelchair?"

The surgeon said, "Possibly. Probably."

We left that office in shock and with instructions that I was not to lift over 5 pounds or to bend from the waist. I knew this was impossible. My baby was nine pounds at birth! I knew I did not know much about God, but I remembered enough from my childhood Sunday School lessons to know that this was not how He operated. I could not imagine that He would not allow me to lift and care for my baby.

I determined then that I would always follow the doctor's instructions faithfully, except when it came to my baby. I tried to do as little lifting as possible, but I held my baby as much as I wanted. I tried to do this while I was seated and I tried to be sensible, but I refused to let this injury keep my baby from feeling the love a baby needs from being held in the arms of his mother.

I was sure God was affirming me in my decision to hold and lift my son, but my confidence was shaken a bit when my husband and I separated. I had no idea how I would raise a child with no one there to help me with all the tasks that come with young children; but my son and I had a joyous time and were always able to do what we needed or God would provide a neighbor or a friend from church to help.

Over the years, I have wound up in the hospital from bending over to put on a pair of pants, from bending to push down lightweight bakery boxes in the trash, and from other thoughtless acts, but I never once was injured by lifting my baby. Today, I walk better than I did then, and it has been twenty-six years since my injury. Praise God! So if you have no idea how your health and your future can possibly work out for your good, I am here to tell you God can overcome any set of circumstances.

God says:

Be strong and courageous. Do not be afraid or terrified because of them, for the Lord your God goes with you; he will never leave you nor forsake you." Deuteronomy 31:6.

You know, I did not have a clear idea of Who God is when all these things happened, and yet I sensed He was near. Something in me just told me that He is good. I did not need to be a Bible expert or in church every Sunday to sense His presence. I now believe there is a part of each of us that just knows there is God with a capital "G."

In the 1600s, Blaise Pascal phrased it this way:

There is a God shaped vacuum in the heart of every man which cannot be filled by any created thing, but only by God, the Creator, made known through Jesus.

Do you ever feel that empty spot that only He can fill? Has your heart been yearning for something more? I encourage you to give God a chance. Reach out to someone you know is a Christian. Or if you are like I was and don't know someone to ask, watch the videos and read the articles at leadingtheway.org where excellent teaching can be found on the Internet or on television. Ask neighbors, co-workers, and acquaintances, but most of all, ask God. He will lead you to a church that teaches the real Christian gospel and not the many knock-offs that people offer these days.

And if you are a Christian and you are not feeling the fullness of his presence as you once did, ask yourself: When was the last time God and you took a vacation together, spent some quality time away from the world together, and that you gave Him your undivided attention for a few days or a week? All relationships blossom with attentiveness, including the intimacy you can grow to have with the Lord.

Determine to spend some time with God, praying, reading your Bible, and asking Him to send people into your life to teach you about Him. He will not disappoint.

IX. ✌ God Is With You in Your Sin and Failure

My greatest earthly failure in my life is my divorce. No matter how hard you have tried to make a marriage work and no matter where the blame may lie, most of us feel a sense of failure at the moment a judge issues that decree that the bond of a marriage is irrevocably broken. At least that is how I felt. Who would have thought that on that day, God would send people to give me encouragement and to let me know He still found me useful to Him?

At the time, I was attending a life-changing Bible Study that is in almost every state and is now international called Bible Study Fellowship or BSF. Bible Study Fellowship is wonderful in that it encourages women to follow God's perfect plan for their lives according to the Bible. Of course, a perfect plan would not include a divorce, but many have made mistakes or have suffered from abuse, infidelity, or even their own mistakes, so sometimes even Christians find they are facing divorce. Still, in BSF we had recently studied that God's will is that marriage be respected and maintained, so I never would have dreamed of what would happen next.

There is a lot of wrong teaching about divorce, but the teaching at BSF is sound. I had received both good and bad teaching in preparation for my divorce. One relative told me, quite incorrectly, that divorce was the unpardonable sin! She could not have been more wrong. God is seen forgiving divorced or adulterous women in the Bible, time after time. I just did not know enough about the

Bible at that time to refute this wrong teaching, but I did seek the opinion of several local pastors.

I made appointments with three pastors known for being against divorce. My husband had been asking for a divorce and the conflict in our home was becoming dangerous. I was especially concerned for what my child was watching and learning from. I went to each pastor and summarized the facts as objectively as I could. Every one told me unhesitatingly that I had grounds for a divorce and assured me I had done all I could to save the marriage. They still felt strongly that divorce is wrong, but they believed the Bible had specific exceptions, and they strongly advised me to give my husband the divorce he wanted. Still, I felt shaky and fearful as I agreed to the process.

I had shared with my BSF small group each step of this process, and I asked them to pray. Finally, it appeared that nothing could stop the process, so I had to get an attorney to protect my child and me and to respond to my husband's attorney. I had very little money, and all I could afford was an attorney who would do a divorce for $325, provided by my American Express legal plan. My husband's family could afford to help him with the fees of a very expensive attorney. He had strong contacts in the legal community because he had been in a position years ago to send these attorneys a great deal of business. If you looked at my situation from a strictly factual perspective, I was outmanned and overpowered. I could not look to any earthly help or high-powered legal team to protect me. Instead, I threw myself on the mercy of the Lord.

To shake my confidence further, had been trying to encourage and record allegations against me. In their calls to people who came into contact with me, they were asking leading questions to try to get people to say terrible things about me. They were trying to say that I was a bad and negligent mother to my son whom I cared for tenderly every day. I had redesigned my whole life to be with my son as much as possible, but that was not the story that was being told about me. Some of the people contacted, who were not personal friends and who were completely objective, called me to tell how unfair the questioning was, and that they felt the caller was trying to put words in their mouths. Instead, most of these people volunteered to testify for me.

In the first book of the Bible, one of God's children tells some people who have tried to harm him, *"As for you, you meant evil against me, but God meant it for good, to bring it about that many people should be kept alive, as they are today." Genesis 50:20 ESV*

That is exactly what happened in my case. This plot to discredit me brought people forth to testify to the evidence they had seen that I was a good mother. I would never have asked for their support, but they volunteered what they had observed when I thought no one was noticing. God is so good.

This was an amazing encouragement personally, but I had no idea how many people had been contacted or if some of my husband's loyal friends might go along with the untrue allegations. My court date was shaping up to have many unknowns stacked against me.

Although my day in court seemed set to be a legal slaughter, I continued to pray to God to handle things for me. I put my life and the result of the legal proceedings in

His hands. I remembered a verse I had learned and felt God was telling me these words were just for me:

This is what the Lord says to you: 'Do not be afraid or discouraged because of this vast army. For the battle is not yours, but God's. II Chronicles 20:15

I truly believed this was God's battle and put it all in His hands and out of mine. I asked that He either heal my marriage and stop the proceedings or that He protect me from this campaign to harm my reputation and take away custody of my child. My only objectives were God's will and what was best for my young child. I was unwilling to fight for the monetary provision beyond the minimums the law provided, though I could have; I just wanted peace and safety.

I had no idea what to expect when our court date finally arrived. I was in constant prayer. The court date happened to land on a day I was to attend BSF. BSF was in the morning and our case was to be heard at 1:00PM. I had just enough time to go to BSF, which was in a northern suburb, and then rush to the downtown Atlanta courthouse for the appointed time. At first, I thought, "I will be so distraught that day that I cannot possibly go and focus on a Bible lesson and a lecture." But I continued to sense that going to hear God's Word that morning was exactly what I needed. I have learned that there is power in the Word that is unexplainable, and in my extremely weak state, I needed that power.

I went to BSF that morning feeling no physical strength, but I felt God's presence holding me up—without a doubt. Although my small group at BSF prayed for me, we stayed focused on the lesson, as I had requested. I was shaky and could not talk about it.

Immediately following the lesson, I rushed to the courthouse, connected with my attorney, and arrived on time. For some reason, my husband was late, so I waited with so many others who were there to have their marriages dissolved by the judge. In a little while, a clerk called my name. I said, "My husband is not here yet." The clerk said, "The judge knows that; he wants to talk to you."

I entered the judge's chambers and was apprehensive that I had perhaps done something wrong. He introduced himself and asked me if my husband and I had attended a required training session for divorcing couples who had children. I told him that we had. I am paraphrasing from memory the conversation that took place next.

"What did you think of it?" asked the judge. I knew that this judge could either be a proponent or a critic of the program as offerings like these were often political. I just had to answer honestly.

I said, "I felt it was beneficial." I then told him a couple of specific takeaways I had from the session.

The judge really warmed up then and began to talk to me with great excitement. He said, "The reason I am asking you is that I saw on these documents that you design training programs for large organizations. What is your opinion of the program as an instructional designer?"

I said, "To serve that many diverse people simultaneously, it does a surprisingly effective job. Time is used efficiently and much information is packed into the short time invested. I was surprised and delighted that the program had some interactivity. So many programs like this just unload too much information without asking the participants to engage. Sure, if money were no object, you could tailor the program more to specific needs, but for people who cannot afford counseling, this program hits all the most important issues. Many of the issues discussed were familiar to my husband and me, but all around me, I heard people making comments that indicated no one had ever taught them these basic parenting principles. It had even more value to them."

The judge by now was grinning with satisfaction. "The reason I asked," he said, "is that this program has been an initiative I have been very involved in. I helped manage the process of developing it. Your group was one of the first to go through it. I really appreciate your feedback."

The moment was surreal. The last thing I could have imagined was that I would be in the judge's chamber helping him evaluate a training program!

Then he said, "You know, this divorce settlement does not provide for your future financially. Although your husband has not had recent sales, his profession is commercial real estate and his potential for income is great. This document says that even if he earns millions, that he never has to pay you or your child more than $20,000 in a year. Normally, I would never agree to a settlement like this but would ask you to go back and take another look at the financial part of this settlement."

One thing I had promised myself from the beginning of our separation and meetings with attorneys had been that my only focus would be on what was best for my child and not on the money. I believed God would take care of us, and there were certain points that were important to me in the raising of my child in a peaceful, safe, and Christ-like manner. The financial part was not a priority.

I said, "Judge, the only thing that is important to me is that I be given custody so I can take care of my child."

He looked at me for a long time and then said, "I can see you are a sensible woman and have been providing well for your child and yourself already. If you are sure you understand that this is not a settlement most women would accept and if you are willing to accept the long term implications, I will grant the divorce."

I told him that the settlement would be acceptable.

He said, "I am granting you full custody." I almost wept with relief. But I still did not understand that the battle was over. I thought I still had to go to court for some official hearing to take place with my husband and his attorney.

The judge said, "No, your husband never showed up, so I have signed the divorce. You and your husband will receive the final decree in about 30 days. Thank you for coming in and talking to me today."

And with that, it was over. No testimony against me, no legal maneuvering, no facing a high paid, intimidating attorney, nothing.

I thought of Psalm 91:7:

A thousand may fall at your side, ten thousand at your right hand, but it will not come near you.

My enemies had simply fallen away.

I know that for a year he had marshaled every force in his power to come against me on this day, but on that day, all that was meant to harm me just evaporated. God does that over and over again. And He can use all kinds of distractions and unlikely things to rescue us. He never does it the way we would have imagined it; He does it better and in a way that, I think, we would have to say could only be God.

The Bible tells the story of many people who have experienced what I felt that day. One is a story of Joshua:

The Gibeonites then sent word to Joshua in the camp at Gilgal: "Do not abandon your servants. Come up to us quickly and save us! Help us, because all the Amorite kings from the hill country have joined forces against us.

So Joshua marched up from Gilgal with his entire army, including all the best fighting men. The LORD said to Joshua, "Do not be afraid of them; I have given them into your hand. Not one of them will be able to withstand you.

After an all-night march from Gilgal, Joshua took them by surprise. The LORD threw them into confusion before Israel, so Joshua and the Israelites defeated them completely at Gibeon. Joshua 10:6-10

Others in history have recorded God defeating their enemies in this same way when they seemed to be outmatched and outnumbered. King Jehoshaphat led Judah at a time when almost everyone was their enemy. Their powerful enemies from Moab, Amnon, and Mount Seir joined forces to destroy Judah. A priest of the Lord told the king, *"Tomorrow march down against them. They will be climbing up by the Pass of Ziz, and you will find them at the end of the gorge in the Desert of Jeruel. You will not have to fight this battle. Take up your positions; stand firm and see the deliverance the LORD will give you,*

Judah and Jerusalem. Do not be afraid; do not be discouraged. Go out to face them tomorrow, and the LORD will be with you."'

Jehoshaphat bowed down with his face to the ground, and all the people of Judah and Jerusalem fell down in worship before the LORD. Then some Levites from the Kohathites and Korahites stood up and praised the LORD, the God of Israel, with a very loud voice.

Early in the morning they left for the Desert of Tekoa. As they set out, Jehoshaphat stood and said, "Listen to me, Judah and people of Jerusalem! Have faith in the LORD your God and you will be upheld; have faith in his prophets and you will be successful.

Then the king did something that showed he truly had confidence that the Lord was going to deliver his people. He told them to start praising!

After consulting the people, Jehoshaphat appointed men to sing to the LORD and to praise him for the splendor of his holiness as they went out at the head of the army, saying:

> *'Give thanks to the LORD,*
> *for his love endures forever.'*

As they began to sing and praise, the LORD set ambushes against the men of Ammon and Moab and Mount Seir who were invading Judah, and they were defeated. The Ammonites and Moabites rose up against the men from Mount Seir to destroy and annihilate them. After they finished slaughtering the men from Seir, they helped to destroy one another.

So to make it perfectly clear, the enemies turned on each other and destroyed one another instead of the people of Judah!

When God delivers you from your enemies because you take Him at His Word and trust Him with all of it, He often does far more for you than you even asked for. For Judah, He gave them rest from war for many years afterwards. Even though He defeated only three of Judah's enemies that day, when the other enemies heard of this slaughter, they decided that Judah was too powerful for them to attack. Judah lived in peace for the first time in a long time, safe from all their enemies and not just the three they had prayed about.

So God also says to you, "Do not be afraid! Do not be discouraged!" Though you may not feel like it, start praising.

God added this extra measure of blessing to my life, too, after answering my prayers for the day of my divorce. In the weeks that followed, He continued to shower His mercy on me and show me evidence of His grace in so many ways.

Shortly after my divorce day, I attended the last day of the year for BSF. I still had residual feelings of having failed to live up to God's best, and I would have understood had the leaders been disappointed in me. I talked to few people and just kept to myself in the large assembly of several hundred women. I just listened to the lecturer and was very quiet that day.

When the final prayer was said and we dismissed, I started down the pew where I had been sitting and headed toward an exit. One of the leaders came to me and said, "Do you have a minute to talk to me?" I said, "Of course."

She said, "The other leaders and I have met, and we have something we want you to consider. We have an opening on our leadership team for a children's leader. Would you pray about joining us?"

Even now as I write this, I weep at the grace and mercy in her words and in the actions of that leadership team. These women taught the Word of God, but they also knew the heart of God. Because of this act of kindness, I did not feel less than worthy; rather, I felt more worthy to serve Him. It was a beautiful affirmation. These leaders were loyal to the teachings of God that divorce is not His choice for us because He knows the hurt and the pain that couples and their children will surely suffer as a result. But these women also knew that God describes Himself as compassionate, and He forgives and forgives and forgives. He truly is the God of mercy, and if we face our mistakes and talk to Him with complete honesty, He will forgive us and help us make a fresh start. 1 John 1:9 tells us:

If we confess our sins, he is faithful and just and will forgive us our sins and purify us from all unrighteousness.

And God is unique in that He is the only person I have ever known who can forgive and truly forget. Once He forgives you, that sin is gone.

Psalm 103:11-13 tells us this about God's willingness to completely forget our sins and mistakes:

For as high as the heavens are above the earth,
*   so great is his love for those who fear him;*
as far as the east is from the west,
*   so far has he removed our transgressions from us.*

As a father has compassion on his children,
*   so the LORD has compassion on those who fear him;*

This is what God means by giving us grace. He gives you this insight into how He looks at your mistakes:

"I, even I, am he who blots out your transgressions, for my own sake, and remembers your sins no more. Isaiah 43:25

This is true grace. In God's eyes, once you genuinely admit a mistake to Him and repent of it, then to Him, it is just as if it never happened! That is amazing.

Do you have any fears of condemnation or reproach from people? Read the story of how Jesus approached a woman that an entire town looked down on and see the grace and mercy He extended to her. He will do the same for you. This beautiful story can be found in John 4. Not just the Samaritan woman mentioned in that story believed; John 4:39 says that "many of the Samaritans from that town believed" in Him because of the woman's testimony that "He told me everything I ever did."

If you go to God with your hurts, pain, and rejection, the change in you may be just what God will use to change others as well.

Some people have this image of God as a condemning, stern figure who is impossible to please. All the evidence contradicts that. Not only does He tells us over and over that He will forgive and forget, there is story after story in the Bible where all kinds of people who murder or lie or commit adultery are forgiven and are clearly loved by God. God goes on to use these people as leaders in His kingdom and to share the message of His love with others.

God took my moment of greatest failure and showed me tenderly and clearly that He still loved me and that He could still use me in His work. He let me know I had a future. Here is a promise to you about your future that you can count on:

"For I know the plans I have for you," declares the LORD, "plans to prosper you and not to harm you, plans to give you hope and a future." Jeremiah 29:11

He is a "yes" God. II Corinthians 1:20 ESV tells us:

For all the promises of God find their Yes in him. That is why it is through him that we utter our Amen to God for his glory.

Let God open the door to your hope and your future. Tell Him the desires of your heart. Confess to Him all your sins and mistakes and anything holding you back from a completely honest relationship from Him. He is a loving Father and wants nothing to harm you. You can trust Him. Find your "yes" in Him; you just have to ask Him.

X. ∾👁 God Is With You When You Fear for Your Children

Just when you think you have grown to the place where you can put your life and future in God's hands, along come your children, and this takes trusting God to a whole new level. You can accept that you may have to suffer and wait, but turning over your child to Him knowing that the child may have to suffer until God's plan is worked out is heart-wrenching. Throughout my life as a Christian, I can hear God at every juncture saying, "Do you trust me?" "Do you trust me even with this?" "Do you trust me even if you don't see any evidence or results for a long time?"

I had gotten to the point that I could answer "yes" to each of these questions, but then I became a mother, and the greatest tests of my faith started. The hardest moments in my life have been when He asked, "Do you trust me with your child?"

As I mentioned, because my husband and I first separated when our son Houston was a baby, letting this infant go for visitation was extremely hard. My husband loved our child very much, but he did not take care of himself. In those days, his drinking was a concern since he was a Type 1 diabetic. During the separation, the first two times he came to pick up our child in his car, his blood sugar was so low that I had to bring him in and give him orange juice until he could speak coherently.

God provided some the perfect caregivers during these visits to my husband. Fortunately, my husband lived with his elderly parents, who doted on their only grandchild, and who lived nearby. God's special gift was the family housekeeper, Mary, who was as much a grandmother to him as his natural grandparents. Houston worshipped her, and he visits her to this day because he loves her so much. She was a wise and protective caregiver. And she was and is a mighty woman of God.

But Mary was only there two days a week. Our divorce took a long time, so Houston was walking and active by the time we worked out an official visitation agreement. I was so anxious as Houston left for his first official visit. He was to be with his dad overnight, and I was concerned about the constant vigilance this toddler required. My apprehension about this first visit peaked when I received a call that Saturday morning from Scottish Rite Children's Hospital that I needed to come to the emergency room right away to sign for stitches for my son. I drove to the hospital fearing what I might find, as the medical personnel would give me no details on the phone.

As it turned out, Houston had cut his hands by playing unattended with some fragile crystal balls that sat on a table on the porch of my in-laws' house. He was hurt, but it was not as bad as I had feared.

Shortly after that, on a subsequent visit, I received another call to come to the hospital because Houston needed x-rays and stitches again. This time, he had been playing unattended while my husband played basketball at a friend's house. Houston was sitting in front of a television set watching cartoons inside the house when their dog came running in from the other room and, with no provocation, attacked his face.

I made my second anxious trip to the emergency room within a few short weeks, not knowing what I would find. When I entered the treatment room in the ER and saw my son's mangled face and the jagged rips in his baby flesh, my first thought was that there was no way he would not be disfigured for life. This child had a beautiful face and a lovely complexion, but he sat forlornly on that table in the emergency room and looked entirely different from the baby who had left my home the day before.

I told my former husband, "I know you feel bad about this." God had told me that I was to represent the love of Christ to him and not be angry with him. And I knew I wanted my husband to spend time with his son, whom he loved so much, and to develop a relationship with him. Still, I felt I had to do something as I did not know what might happen next to my child. I wondered if the visitation could be supervised in some way, though I knew my husband would fight that. I contacted attorneys who were family and close friends to ask their advice about possible solutions. One valued advisor had been the judge presiding over the juvenile court in our county and had seen many cases like this. Their advice was discouraging. Not allowing my husband to see his child unsupervised would not be an option. Even if we went to court, these two accidents could be viewed as coincidental—things that just happen when you have young children. Also, if we pursued protecting my child through legal means, my husband would probably cite his diabetes as a reason for not knowing the child was in danger. Even the most conscientious diabetic has low blood sugar sometimes. This lack of care for himself, however, was endangering our son.

I have many close friends with Type 1 diabetes who conduct their business and social lives successfully and whom I would trust my child to unhesitatingly, but this was different. At times, my husband would give himself far more than the recommended dosage of insulin, or he would not time the insulin the way the doctors had taught him. This mismanagement of his insulin had gone on for at least a decade, and he knew the consequences. Still, he continued with the same unhealthy pattern, and at that time, no one could talk him into taking the basic precautions.

I was also told that if I tried to get his visitation supervised some way, that I could be misunderstood; my concern was not that he was a diabetic but a diabetic whose life was complicated by alcohol. I knew pursuing any legal means of protection was futile.

Here I was-- with no source of protection for my child, powerless, and utterly desperate. Having nowhere to turn on earth, I turned to my Heavenly Father. I threw myself at His feet and asked for mercy and protection for my child. I thought He would give me a method of protection, but His answer was one I have heard many times. "Wait and trust in me." WAIT? I could not just wait. My child was in danger. Yet, He quietly continued to tell me to wait. Then it was as if He pulled me up by my lapels and said, "Do you think your child is any safer when his hand is in yours than when his hand is in your husband's? I am the only one who can protect your child. NOT YOU!"

I had a fleeting vision of all the dangers in this world that could happen to a young child or anyone: car accidents, tornadoes, falls. I realized my complete impotence to prevent accidents or disease or harm. I even thought briefly that without the gravity God provided, my child and all of us would go flying off the face of the earth. We were all completely dependent on God for each breath and for our daily safety. I got it. Finally, I understood that I HAD to release my son, not to my husband's care, but to God's care. And that is exactly what I did. It was the hardest thing I ever had to do, but I told God that I was not going to fight, not going to try to enforce what I thought best, but that I was turning my child completely over to Him. I was placing this tiny child into His hands for His protection. And the accidents stopped immediately.

Not all the fears we have for our children are for their physical protection. Sometimes the emotional and psychological threats can hold the potential for more long-term damage.

When Houston was about six, he encountered a person when he was not in my care who was abusive to him psychologically and emotionally. Houston also felt this person was putting him into harm's way physically. He told of being at the pool, and how two older boys were allowed to hold his head under water for long periods of time while this adult crouched at the side of the pool and looked into his eyes each time he came up gasping for air. My son was a very active, rough and tumble guy whose friends and he often played dunking games, so he was unafraid of normal horseplay. This was different. The terrified child told me later, "Mommy, I thought I was going to die."

Sadly, I did not know of this abuse at first because it did not happen when I was around. My son was threatened, as abusers often do, not to tell anyone of the many horrific things that had happened to him. When my son finally told another child on the playground at school, that wise playmate went home and told his parents. I will be forever grateful, because the school called in all parties involved and demanded counseling to help my son through this ordeal. The truth came out. The person then tried to threaten me that I would be sued for slander for what my child had said. Remember that I had not even known about this until the school had called me, so these charges were ridiculous. My attorney responded for me to these threats and, in fact, welcomed the opportunity to explore in court what had taken place. My accuser backed down immediately. Still, I do not want to share the details here as it is not my goal to harm this person. My son is a strapping twenty-seven-year-old now, and the things this hurt and damaged person did then could not happen now. He is safe.

Still, until all the details were worked out, it appeared that my son might have to encounter this person again from time to time. He was sick with dread. Several things happened that alleviated that dread somewhat. First, the person took a long trip abroad. This provided immediate relief my son badly needed. I could say, "That person is not even in this country."

When the abuser returned, there was still incentive for them to avoid my son as they were under scrutiny and had a lot to lose. When later my son had to run into them occasionally, it was uncomfortable, but he now understood the power he had to get help from the school and, of course, me. He was unafraid of their threats now that they had been exposed as lies, powerless against my son now.

One day, when we realized that my son might have to encounter his abuser and there was no way to avoid it, I had to go to him and talk to him about it. I purchased a beautiful painted box. I told him, "All your life, I have been able to solve all your problems. Now I have to tell you that you may run into this person when you are not with me, and I can't stop it. I know you are safe, but I also know you do not want to see them at all. I would give anything if I could fix this. This is the first thing in your life that Mommy can't fix. So when you can't handle something and I can't handle something, we have to take the big problems to God. He can handle it. We are going to write our prayer requests for things we can't handle, and we are going to put them in this box. God will answer them. He will help you. And one day, when you are older, we will open this box up and see how God answered every prayer."

For the time being, however, it was a terrible time in his life. My son had always been the most joyous, highly active, outgoing child at his school. He loved everyone and loved to play boisterously. When these terrifying things first occurred, he became very subdued. I tried to comfort him and to assure him we were protecting him, but his emotional wounds were deep and would need time to heal. I even took him on a trip with his cousins that he most loved to play with. They would head out to play and he would just lie there in the fetal position. We had exposed what was happening but now he felt he could just collapse.

Before, he had forced himself to carry on because he had been threatened. Now he just fell apart; he had lost his usual spunk. All the fight was gone.

During the first few weeks, he wanted to be in my presence constantly. I was by his side comforting him and felt this was entirely appropriate for a time. But as the weeks passed, I realized that I was becoming far too important to him. He needed to cling to me at first, but we needed now to slowly strengthen him and restore his wonderful independent spirit. I did not want to become a focal point for him. I have seen other single moms do this, and it is not good for a child long term.

I began to try to think of something he wanted very much, outside of activities with me. My son was always precocious, and he had once asked me if he could attend a very expensive private school in Atlanta, a long drive from the Marietta suburb where we lived. Both the expense and the commute were too much for this working mom the first time he had asked. Now, I was willing to do anything to get him excited about something besides activities with me, and no expense or effort was too much.

I did not know anything about getting a child into this school, Westminster. All my life I had heard of this nationally recognized school, and the rumor mill had it that you had to have recommendations from the most stellar people in the community and that unless you were an alum or had a sibling there already, getting in was nigh impossible.

I then realized that there was no way we could get him in for the following year, as it would take me a year to strategize and network to get friends of friends to seek the recommendations needed. That was good, because as reality sank in, I realized that there was no way I could transport him there morning and afternoon from our suburb and get myself to work. Maybe in a year or two I could move closer. What I could offer my child was to work through the application process that year just to learn the ropes. We needed to stop depending on rumors and find out exactly what was required to get in for some future year. I was honest with my elementary school age son that this year was a learning year, but that we would take steps to get him in for junior high school or high school. I had found out that the school created more spaces at the junior high school level and even more for high school, making the chances of acceptance greater.

I was told that most people who start their children at Westminster at age five do so because of the fine academics. They will not give that slot up for almost any reason. Because of this, only a few slots open up later in elementary school, and there are scores of applicants.

So I filled out the forms, and because it was just a learning year, I did not bother to get any recommendations beyond the minimum required: my son's principal and one coach. After all, this was just an exercise, right?

When Houston and I went to Westminster for his group interview, I was daunted by the library packed with applicants. And this was just one cohort of applicants; others were scheduled to come on other days! Every student and his mother that I talked to had at least one other sibling at Westminster already. Friends had told me that those students with siblings would be admitted first. Since we were told there were only three openings that year, that booted my son out of the running. But we still wanted to go through the exercise to learn how to do this process better when the time came.

My son completed his interview, we got the required testing submitted, and I thought that was that.

One Saturday morning, I eased down my driveway to take Houston to his baseball game and decided to grab up my mail as I went so I could read it during inning changes. On top, I saw the letter from Westminster. I decided to go ahead and open it there in the car. I was in shock when I saw that Houston had been admitted to the class that would start in just a few months. My first feeling was elation. My second was dismay. Where would the money come from? How could I overcome the logistics of getting him there and back each day? It was impossible. I paused for a moment to pray, but I will admit I went to the game in a stupor.

I did not want to talk to anyone, as I needed to think, really think. I sat away from the crowd and asked God what did He want? I knew immediately that sending Houston to Westminster was His will, so I asked God to show me how to do it.

Then a woman who attended our church came up and told me her son had been admitted to Westminster in the same grade! I had not even known he had applied. She could not carpool because she had four children and all her seatbelts were taken, but I felt encouraged. Houston would be starting with a friend he had played sports with and gone to church with.

When I got home that afternoon, I was telling a neighbor about my joyous dilemma. She said, "I think the Abbots (fictitious name) go to Westminster, and those boys are close to Houston's age." Now let me tell you how bizarre this is. I had been extremely active in my neighborhood for years, even heading up the playgroup for a while. Even though we had 140 homes, I thought I knew all the young boys. Now someone was mentioning a family I had never heard of!

I called this family immediately and confirmed that these children were attending Westminster. I asked the mom if she would be interested in carpooling. Here is what she said, "I will on one condition. I want my nanny to do all the driving. She has little to do and this would work best for my children's activities. I have been needing to solve a problem and your call is the answer. My nanny has to go to her doctor from time to time, and I have no backup for those days or for sick days or vacations. If you can just be my back up for those days, I would be delighted. My husband and I are both physicians, and we have difficulty covering if the nanny calls in sick or needs to go somewhere."

I got off the phone stunned. God had just provided a perfect carpool that would require very little driving time for me! What were the odds of that? That was my first miracle of the day.

The next issue was money. I called my former husband who had been asked by his girlfriend at one time not to contribute to private school, although he had agreed to do so at the time of the divorce. I said, "Out of respect for your role as father, I am letting you know that Houston has been accepted at Westminster. I know you have said you would no longer contribute to private school, but I felt I should tell you about this and give you the opportunity if you choose to be a part of this. I am not asking you for money and will find a way to finance it. I will tell you, however, that I have never known Houston to want something so much. You know he never asks for toys or electronics or a new bike. This is the first thing I can ever remember that he has asked for. I am letting you know in case you want to be a part of it."

After some consideration, he called me back to say he would pay for half. That was my second miracle.

The third miracle was that I landed a lucrative project that made the funding of my half possible without borrowing any money. God did all of this within 24 hours!

God is the God of the impossible. When you fear for your child, ask God for His help because He can solve your problems in ways you won't see coming.

So here is the most wonderful part of this second story. Houston went on to love Westminster, and it was the perfect school for him. A smart, fun, great group of boys took him under wing from the first day and included him in activities and birthday parties and recreational sports. That same group of boys (and their fantastic parents) are like family to him even today, though they have been out of college and in their careers for a few years. Their love for each other is tempered by large doses of hilarity. They stay in contact through a text "thread"; they visit each other in the many cities from New York to San Francisco where they are all working; and they provide tremendous support for each other.

Shortly before Houston graduated from high school, he and I opened up the God Box where we had put in that first sad prayer request over twenty years ago. Then, we could not possibly see how God could turn the terrible experience he had gone through as a young child into something that would bless him for the rest of his life. We realized that if I had not been desperate to do something to pull him out of his funk back then, that I never would have done something so impractical as apply to a school I could not afford. This gut-wrenching experience led to one of the greatest blessings of Houston's life. This only child has five friends who are truly like brothers to him, and they never would have met if I had not been looking for a fresh start for him.

So often God works that way. He takes our pain and somehow reworks our lives so that we and others are blessed through it.

One event at Westminster was not a good memory. When my son was a sophomore, he was taking the PSAT one day when he fell out of his desk in a seizure-like state that terrified his young teacher. He writhed on the ground for minutes, and no one could stop the shaking for a long time. The teacher called me and told me what violent physical tremors and other symptoms my son had experienced. I rushed to the school and took him straight to our beloved but straight-talking pediatrician, a brilliant diagnostician often consulted by the CDC on difficult cases. Dr. Steven Shore has a reputation for being able to find the answer even when others have failed, but for the first time in fifteen years, he did not have the answer.

In his usual direct style, he told me, "It is either neurological or cardio. We may not have a lot of time to figure this out, so I recommend we check him out for cardio issues first; those can kill him faster." He made a call to Sibley Heart Center where one of the best pediatric cardiologists in the nation was on staff.

On the way to the Center, I became even more alarmed because my son confessed he had had a couple of these episodes and had not told me about them. This macho fifteen year old told me, "I actually feel good after them. I am not sick. I knew you would make a big deal out of this."

We signed in at the desk and were soon taken back for a barrage of all kinds of tests. At the end of the testing, I asked the technician, "Do you have any results?" He said, "Oh no. It will take the doctors two weeks to study all this and to make a diagnosis. You will probably even have to come back for more tests before a final diagnosis is made."

My heart fell. What if the next episode were fatal? I was about to walk out with no more help for my son than when I walked in. I went through the motions of getting our bill and walking to the checkout station in a stunned state.

I will always be grateful that an insurance question kept us at the checkout desk an unusually long time that day. After the drawn out process, we were headed to the exit when the nurse came running after us and said, "Wait! The doctor wants to talk to you."

She took us back to his office, not an exam room, but his private office. He said, "I was not even supposed to come in today, but I needed some data for a paper I was writing and came into my office to get it off the computer. I happened to see your file on top of a stack to be reviewed next week. I see that your son has exactly the symptoms of the condition I have been writing about. There is no need to wait; I can tell you exactly what your son has, neurocardiogenic syncope."

Though I was flooded with gratitude that God had put Houston's file before this expert and given us a diagnosis, the condition sounded terrifying.

The doctor went on, "And it does not require surgery. In fact, the treatment is fairly simple, but it will take six months and does have side effects. But at the end of six months, your son will probably be fine and will never have another episode again."

Now that sounded better. We started Houston on the medication that day, and he never had another episode again.

I can never express my gratitude for all the "coincidences" that led to this accurate and swift diagnosis. What if I had gone to another doctor whose focus was not on this rare condition? What if the doctor had not come in that day to get the data he had left behind? We could have gone through months of testing and perhaps more damaging episodes before we got this correct diagnosis.

When Adam and Eve broke the rules of the Garden of Paradise, we went from living in a disease-free, pain-free world where everything was provided for us to the very difficult existence we live now. God did not bring illness into the world; MANKIND did. Yet God in His mercy comes along side us to comfort us in our illnesses and to provide doctors and healing for us. He does not leave us alone in our difficult circumstances.

He is the other parent with you when you have urgent health decisions to make about your child, and unlike you, He is a perfect parent. This is especially comforting if you are a single parent. If you pray, He will direct you to the right path to a solution.

Many verses and stories in the Bible reveal a tenderness in God's heart toward children. He gives them a type of understanding and comfort we mortals can rarely achieve.

"...but Jesus said, "Let the little children come to me and do not hinder them, for to such belongs the kingdom of heaven." Matthew 19:14

He cares for your child even more than you do, if you can imagine that. He will do what is best for your child. Just as there are times you have to allow your child to not understand the reasons for the things you do, so God sometimes has a good plan for your child that does not make sense at the time. Trust Him the way you want your children to trust you. He can be relied on to make decisions based on past, present and future information. You only have past and present information. He will make the decision that will bless your child most.

XI. God Is With You in Your Service to Him in Your Church

Service to the Lord has brought me some of the greatest joy and satisfaction in my life. There are moments when you are serving in a role the Lord has drawn you to that you have a contentment and energy that are far better than enjoying your secular work. Most Christian service involves others, and the fellowship and deepening relationships through service are a major blessing. When we bless others, we are blessed in ways we could not have anticipated.

But at times, your service will come at a cost. I have come to believe that when service is difficult or costly, it makes our gift more precious to Him.

I am a big believer in not overthinking service to the Lord too much. If your brother and sister in front of you is in need, there is a good chance you are called to help them. Compassion, charity and love should be our impulse if we are truly seeking to follow Christ. Major commitments to long-term service, however, require more prayer. In our busy churches today, you may be offered many different opportunities for service, and certainly you can serve in several ways simultaneously. I serve on a prayer team, but I also serve as mentor in a program for our young women, and in a couple of other roles. But I am not called to do everything everyone asks me to do, nor are you. Figuring out the major service commitments you are to make takes a great deal of prayer, and His choice may surprise you.

I have done seminars and taught at the college level for forty years, so I assumed that when I committed my life to Him, He would have me teach a Sunday School class or a Bible study. But in my prayer time, I did not feel He was drawing me there at all. Though more recently I have taught an occasional breakout session or Lunch & Learn, teaching is not my ongoing service at my church. Primarily, prayer has been. It is a hidden ministry and so unlike the public seminars I conduct in my business. God let me know He does not need my earthly gifts; He wants my obedience to do the tasks He has chosen for me.

I learned the hard way over twenty years ago that taking on a role God had not chosen for me was not good for me or for the people I would serve. God only had to show me this lesson once; it was so painful at the time, that I have never forgotten it. I am so grateful for all I learned back then about asking God for His guidance about service, but I would not want to relive those enlightening months.

When my son Houston was seven, we were very active in our local church, but we were still getting to know all the wonderful people and programs after our move from our old church. One day, we were walking down a hallway and saw a sign for an activity that was a game-based approach to learning Scripture. It promised to teach children more about the Bible in a fun style using a team approach for friendly competition. Both Houston and I were excited about this idea, and I called to ask how to sign him up to participate.

The young leader of volunteers said, "I am sorry. We don't have a group for the younger kids. At this time, we only have a group for middle and high school children that I teach. I have been considering teaching one myself for this age group, but I just have to figure out if I have the time to take on another group. Would you be interested in leading the group?"

I said, "I wish I could, but that would be impossible. I am doing other volunteer work, and honestly, I am struggling right now to be a single mom and breadwinner and take my son to all his activities. We are going through a difficult time, but God is helping us through it."

A few days later, she called to say that she was establishing a group for the younger children. We would have our first informational meeting Sunday after church. Houston was so excited.

When we walked into the meeting a few minutes late, parents were having an informal time of conversation. One of the other parents with whom I had worked in the nursery came up and said, "When I heard you were going to lead this Bible study activity, I signed my children up."

I was shocked. I thought she had misheard. I headed over toward the leader of volunteers who immediately told the group, "This is Casey Hawley who will be leading the elementary age group."

I was stunned. I did not want to embarrass her, so I decided to wait until I could talk to her privately so I could tell her again that there was no way I could do this. In the meantime, several parents I loved came to me to express their gratitude and to affirm me. I was cordial in return, but I was very confused.

I took the leader aside for a moment and told her how overwhelmed with life I was right now and that I could not do this. I asked if she had misunderstood my earlier "No."

She laughed and said, "I understood, but I think you will do fine." I continued trying to explain my inability to do this, but she continued to say, "Just do it for a while. I think you will like it."

I finally was very direct and said, "I am not saying "I won't; I am saying I can't."

She was annoyed and said, "Just do it for the first meeting or two until I can call around and get someone else."

I was happy to help out for a week or two, and agreed to that. As the meeting progressed, I was also dismayed to find out that this activity required competing with different churches, some several hours away. The problem with that was that the competitions were on Saturdays. Saturday was my day to do what all the stay-at-home moms did on Monday through Friday. Saturdays made life possible. Taking away my catch-up day threw me into a panic. My life was barely working now, and to lose some Saturdays needed for major housecleaning, errand running, and other chores threatened near collapse. None of this had been included in the flyer.

Still, I thought, I can make it through two weeks. But though I continued to call the leader of volunteers to see if she were pursuing someone else to lead, she just continued to say that she would give me materials and websites to help me do it. I could not make my voice heard.

I had a bad feeling about what was happening from the beginning. As the weeks dragged on, I continued to ask God if He had changed His mind, but I consistently sensed He was not calling me to this particular service.

The delightful part of this story is that the children were precious; I loved each and every one of them. It was challenging, however, because I had a group of mostly young (six year old) shy girls and a bunch of big (eight and nine) hyperactive boys who were very loud. The boisterous boys did not mean to intimidate the girls, but unfortunately, they did. I asked God to show me what to do. As long as I was there, I wanted to help make this a good experience for these young ones.

God gave me very clear direction. Even though I had been given a very structured format to follow, He told me to carve out time to add a prayer time in the beginning. He led me to teach the children to pray for one another. It is very hard to be intimidated by someone you are praying for.

Each week, we would spend about ten minutes talking about our prayer requests for that week. These sweet children asked for prayer for sick grandparents, for their spelling tests, and for all sorts of things in their lives. We would then pray for God to teach us about His Word through the lesson and game we were about to participate in. Then I encouraged them to pray for one another, and I prayed too. The children quickly became a sweet prayer group, supporting each other's needs. Then we would move on to the game. I knew that there had been a comment that we were not following the structure exactly by using some practice time for prayer, but I knew God was pleased.

I continued to call the leader of volunteers to see if she could put another volunteer in my place, but she just said, "See if you can find someone to do it." I tried. I asked the other parents, but they were too busy. I wanted to reach out to others in the church, but we were still relatively new, and I did not know anyone to ask.

As we approached the first Saturday competition, I did not know what to expect. Since I had never seen a match, I did not know how our children would hold up in the intense competition. My little girls on the team were just the most delicate flowers I had ever seen and were of particular concern to me. Some of the churches we were competing against had children who had been quizzed on the same questions for seven years. We barely had seven weeks in! This competition was one of the big ones, with many churches participating. I hoped our children would not become discouraged.

In the two weeks leading up to our first competition, the enemy did all he could to discourage me. First, we had a major house fire and were forced to move out of our home for months. The experience had shaken me, and getting to all of our activities and carpools from our hotel miles away was just not working. Each day, I was exhausted even when I woke up and had to juggle so many new problems and hire contractors and make decisions while working more than forty hours a week and spending quality time with Houston. I went to the leader of volunteers and said, "I really cannot continue to lead this group with all these burdens from the fire. Would you please get some of the other parents to do it?" She did not respond. I also let the other parents know that we were now struggling even more and that I needed help. There was silence.

The same weekend we had our fire, another family in our church had a fire as well. This was one of the most wonderful families, and later I got to know and love them well. Even at the time, my heart went out to them as I knew what they were suffering. There is no such thing as a less serious fire, but their damage was not as extensive as that on my home, and they were not going to be vacated as long. Each week, as the volunteer leader brought her child to our classroom and greeted her friends in the class, she would be arranging help for this family, coordinating meals, and expressing concern for the other family's difficult living circumstances as parents brought their children into my room. The other family deserved all the concern and support given, and they were gracious and humble in the way they accepted it, but the complete omission of even an expression of concern for us seemed pointed. This is how our enemy works on Christians. He wants to divide us over things like this. It was evident that this was a tactic to divide us and keep both of us from mutually showing the love of Christ to one another. Divisions in the body of Christ happen all the time over small hurts like this. Knowing the source of this unkindness really helped me as I served these adults every week; serving their children was a joy.

Only one parent ever said to me they were sorry for what we were walking through, and no one ever offered a meal or help. As a single mom, I have found there are three types of people based on how they respond to single moms. By far the most prevalent way is that most people are kind, compassionate, and thoughtful. I could write a book on the intuitive ways Christian women have realized how my singleness might make a situation hard for me with no husband there and have gone out of their way to be there for me. Their husbands have put together my toys at Christmas, given my son lessons in shooting hoops, and made sure my son had someone looking out for him in baseball leagues. This is the majority.

The second type is the person who has no awareness that singleness may bring challenges. These are caring and valued people, but as they plan school or social events, they assume everyone has a partner at home. I love these people, and they are innocent in any decisions they make that might be difficult for single parents. Sometimes I even like not being differentiated, so I am also blessed by this type.

By far the minority is the small group of people who, for whatever reason, are uncomfortable with single parents. Their discomfort may take the form of exclusivity, awkwardness, condemnation, or downright hostility. I do understand some of the sources of this discomfort. Children from single parent homes may have more discipline problems or other issues if at least one of the parents is not a strong and loving force in that child's life. It takes a monumental effort to support a family and simultaneously give a child all the attention he would receive in a two-parent household, so some children of single parent homes do not receive all the attention they crave.

Another reason for this occasional prejudice against single parents is that our sin is public. We should never have gotten ourselves into a situation leading to divorce. And if a married Christian woman has a tendency toward the sin of self-righteousness, it is very easy for the enemy to tempt her to unintentionally or intentionally shun a divorced woman. And truthfully, even in my case where I was told I had Biblical grounds, I was still at fault. Decisions I made long before I ever met my husband led me to choose a husband that was not walking with the Lord. We did not have the marriage God wanted because we were not independently living the lives God wanted us to live when we decided to get married—neither of us.

Another reason for some to shun single moms, I've been told, is that for some women we bring up unconscious fears that something like this could happen to them. And finally, there are still some women who are wary of single moms being included in family activities because of the possibility that a single woman may tempt a husband into adultery. This seems strange to me in this day when, sadly, so many affairs are occurring between married people, even in the church, but I do know this fear exists.

All this to say that the body of Christ that I was exposed to during this very difficult season in my life included a couple of moms from this third type. They may even have felt they had Biblical grounds. Because of exhaustion, I began to have health issues. As I began to have these health problems, as I struggled to drive many miles every day because of not being able to live in my own neighborhood for months, and as I walked through one difficulty after another, I sensed they felt that I had brought my difficult life on myself and did not deserve a kind word or support. I did not expect to be invited to the social events they talked freely about in front of me that included most of the parents in the class but not me. After all, I was not just a single mom, I was an older mom, and relatively new to the church. I understood that, but did not want my son to suffer for these differences.

When I prayed, the Lord let me know clearly that the enemy would love for me to get my mind fixed on my difficulties and the unkind treatment. He told me that this is exactly how our enemy works in churches to stir up ill feeling and to make people less effective in working together to achieve what He wants. He told me that even if I never received one thing back from my church, I was to love my church and every single person in it. Loving our friends and people who help us is easy; loving people who despitefully use us is loving like Christ. When we were callous and unloving to God, He loved us anyway. He even gave His only Son for us. We are to love like God loves, unselfishly; so I determined to be loving toward these people and serve them with all the kindness I could until I could find my way out of this service He never planned for me. God is a God of order, and I needed to make this transition in the right way.

The week before we went to the competition, my son found out that all of the other children were riding a bus to the match that was several hours away. He was terribly hurt that he had not been included. Riding a bus may not sound like a lot of fun to us adults, but to young kids who had never taken a road trip, this was an exciting prospect they were all talking about. One of the moms had arranged for the bus and had let all the parents know about it but me. My son cried and I was so sorry for him; still, I continued to ask Jesus to give me peace in my heart and the ability to show love in my words and actions.

Two days before the competition, I came down with what I found out later was strep throat, and on that Saturday, I went to the competition with a 103° fever. I had called to see if someone else could handle the meet, but there were no suggestions, even though most of the parents were going to the meet.

We made the long drive to the host church. Various children from my team competed in different rooms in different buildings on their campus. I was physically so weak as I went from room to room encouraging the children and reminding them how we had been praying for each other to be brave and to depend on God to help us today. Some of these children had been so shy that only recently had they been able to answer the questions out loud in our little practice room at our home church. I prayed God would give them boldness and courage.

We did not win the competition, but we definitely put points on the board and were respectable. When it was over, leaders from many different churches came up to me and said they had never seen a new team do as well in a first competition. The questions are asked at a lightning fast speed, and buzzers cut the children off if they are not quick. I was told this first experience shakes most children up the first time, and they never even answer a question. The first match is considered a learning experience, and no one is expected to put points on the board. Not only were our children answering, in some cases they were winning points against more experienced churches. These courageous young ones had spoken up and been able to answer some of the questions without being shaken by the loud sounds and pressure of the competition.

As I saw them afterwards, I reminded them that God had done this for them and that their prayers for each other had been answered. I was thanking God in my heart that the children had not had to suffer for my disobedience in serving where He had not called me.

I went home knowing several things. First, I knew I was not a game or competition coach and that the only reason we were respectable that day was because the prayers of the children had been answered. Second, I knew that I was being disobedient by continuing a service He had tried to close the door to for me. Third, I needed to focus on the ministries He had called me to, take care of my child while we were living like gypsies out of a hotel room, and regain the peace of my household.

I went home and wrote a loving letter of resignation, but I made it clear that Houston and I would not be in the room the next Sunday; if the class were to go on, some other parent would need to supervise. At this point, Houston did not want to go back. The activity had not been as challenging as he had thought, since he already knew a great deal of Scripture from his Bible Study Fellowship class. I offered him the option of staying and participating, but it had not been a fit for him either. Soon after, we found out that a Bible Study Fellowship group in a nearby suburb had an evening program for children Houston's age. He was ecstatic to join that as his activity to study the Bible.

Galatians 1:10 says, "Am I now trying to win the approval of human beings, or of God? Or am I trying to please people? If I were still trying to please people, I would not be a servant of Christ."

I was clearly trying to please people when I should have had blinders on to all else but pleasing God. At that first meeting, I had not wanted to contradict the leader in front of the crowd, and I did not want to disappoint people who were complimenting and affirming me. My pride was a bit puffed up by the nice things people were saying. I did not want to seem unpleasant or let people down as the weeks progressed, and I disobediently spent many hours on something I was not called to. The result was that I neglected the ministry I was called to.

My very wise friend Frances Pastore shared with me a devotional from Oswald Chambers on this subject. In his soul-nourishing book my *Utmost for His Highest*,

Chambers has an incredible devotional entitled "What My Obedience to God Costs Other People." He says, *"If we obey God, it is going to cost other people more than it costs us, and that is where the pain begins."* I found that to be so true in this experience.

In the end, the activity went on, and I learned a valuable lesson about listening and obeying God. When faced with my firm resignation, other parents stepped forward. Often when we are doing a ministry we are not called to do, we prevent someone God is calling from serving in that place. This experience has made me enter into any long-term service commitment more prayerfully.

God taught me the way He wants me to approach any major commitment to service and that He has very specific plans for me. To this day, I benefit from this experience, and it has led me to such joyful service. When we do the service He calls us to, there is a deep satisfaction and peace that is difficult to explain. I appreciate that feeling each time I sense it, because I know what it feels like to be out of His will and not feel that peace. Even the hard lessons bring us joy eventually.

When I pray with the women I meet with each Wednesday at 4:30PM, I feel that joy and peace. Our service is to pray for the women of our church, their health, their salvation, their walk with the Lord, and their futures. We pray about the Women's Ministry and for God's guidance on what Bible studies to offer, what events we should do to save the lost and equip the saints, and what God's vision is for the future. This has been the right service for me for eight years, and it will be right until God draws me to the next opportunity for service. Sometimes a type of service is for a season in your life; as you enter a new season, He may want you to move to a different form of service.

Other ways I have served have cost me what is most precious for me to give up—my time; but it has been amazing how God has expanded my time and has gone ahead of me to take care of many tasks so that the time is not missed—as long as I am in His will. The more I give to service, it seems the more I am blessed. This seems impossible, but I have talked to other Christians who say it is their experience too. I would say to those who feel God is calling them to a service but they don't see how they will find the time, STEP FORWARD IN FAITH. You will experience an amazing demonstration of how God can do impossible things in your life. Don't miss this supernatural display of His power.

The key to it all is prayer. Holding everything up to God in prayer will keep you aligned with His plan for your time and your life. Studying and reflecting on the Bible will further open your eyes to His will for you. Trust Him.

XII. 🐚 God Is With You When You Think He Isn't Paying Attention to Your Loneliness and Loss

Have you ever wondered if God has lost your contact information? If He has taken His eye off you? If He, with all His billions of children, has somehow forgotten you? I felt that way in a very difficult period from 2011 until 2013. In my heart and head, I knew God had not forgotten me, and I knew emotions are unreliable. Still, we sometimes can't help the irrational feelings we have, especially if a season of loneliness lasts a long time.

This season of loss in my life began when my charming, funny, larger-than-life mother died of Alzheimer's in November. They call this disease "The Long Goodbye" for good reason. The mother I knew and, more importantly, who once knew me, had been gone for a long time. Though I was happy she was celebrating and healthy in Heaven, losing this indescribably important person in my life left a huge, gaping hole. I was actively grieving for months.

In July of 2013, my best friend died. Our lives had been so interwoven and we were always talking on the phone or in person throughout the week. She was not just my friend; she was the Women's Ministry Director at our church, and we worked on almost every event at the church together, prayed together, and talked on the phone at the end of the day and sometimes throughout the day. We were in meetings at our church together frequently, and saw each other several times a week. My son usually came home on major holidays, but minor ones like Memorial Day or even

July 4th usually found me alone. She and her husband included me in festive cookouts and dinners, so I never felt alone on those very family-oriented days. Belinda Stone was extraordinary, not just in my eyes but to anyone who ever met her. Her funeral drew people from all over our city, and everyone agreed there was no one like this greatly admired leader and Christ-like woman. To lose any friend is hard, but to lose someone so exceptional makes the loss staggering,

I had been asked to give a eulogy at Belinda's funeral, and was weak with grief afterwards. As I drove out of the parking lot, I received a call from Hospice that my sister Jan was not going to live through the night. If I wanted to see her, I should come. Jan had been diagnosed with cancer six years before when I had made this baby sister of mine go to the doctor with a suspicious lump in her breast. I was the one person who was with her for every surgery, emergency room visits for infected ports or dangerous white blood counts, and many chemo appointments that followed in the next six years. Various friends came and went in those six years, but we were constants in one another's lives.

Jan was divorced as I was, and we would often spontaneously run out to a movie on Friday nights or go eat sushi on our lunch hours or go shopping. She and I shared a passion for looking for hidden gems at the many Goodwill stores in metro Atlanta. We called these treasure hunts "Goodwill Hunting." Though Jan was eight years younger, we had the same sense of humor and similar skills in our careers, so we understood each other. Jan was a restaurant reviewer for an online service, so her lunch tab was paid for, though she was not well paid. Once or twice a week, she would ask me to meet her so we could try out a new restaurant and she could write the review. Though usually nothing could pry me from my downtown Atlanta office for even a quick sandwich, after Jan got cancer, I would drive the fifteen to twenty miles to her territory for reviews, and we would experiment with new restaurants. I felt that if I would agree to meet her, she would eat, and encouraging her to eat had been a challenge. This strategy worked for a very long time. We filled a void in each other's lives and saw each other often. At the end of Jan's life, some of her generous-hearted college friends came forward and cared for her, but for a long season before that, I was the sole person in her support system. You become very close to someone you serve like that, so I became even more attached to her in those years. Her death left empty spots throughout my week and in my heart. I had now lost the two people I saw every week, the people who were my running buddies, and who had warded off loneliness for me for many years.

Even though the loss of Jan and Belinda had been anticipated, the deaths still sent me reeling. Because they happened so close together, I felt hit by a double whammy.

Not all great losses are through death. The final loss in my life came as a complete surprise. My wonderful son, who is bright and conversational and funny, had made a practice of coming home from college fairly frequently in his junior and senior years. After he had gotten over his first two years of feeling he had to attend every frat and sorority party on campus, rarely coming home except for Christmas and Thanksgiving, he settled down and enjoyed a more balanced social life. On his trips home, we enjoyed great conversations, coffee by the river, and dinners with friends. He could drive home after class on Friday and we could have a late dinner at Willie's, his favorite Mexican place. We enjoyed many visits in those years.

My son had consistently had a career focus on finance and had completed several related internships. In his senior year, he had job offers from major investment firms and was trying to make up his mind. During this process, he was invited to interview with a start-up high tech company from the Silicon Valley. He went to the interview because he was impressed about how much the recruiter had known about him, and Houston was intrigued but not really interested in the job. Houston actually laughed at the idea that he would work for a software-related company based in California; my very conservative son had never been a techie at all, and this young Republican who was already politically active did not see the west coast as a place where he would thrive. But the company was looking for raw intelligence. They gave math tests to be calculated in the candidate's head and questions were of this nature: "If we shrunk you to the size of a nickel and put you in a blender, how would you get out?"

Houston was fascinated by the people, but he still laughed at the idea of working in the cyber-security industry. He continued to go on subsequent interviews because he just found the process so interesting.

Then one day, he called and said, "Mom, I can't believe I am saying this, but I am actually considering taking this job."

Everything in me said, "Noooooooo!" Before I could answer Houston, my first thoughts were, "Oh Lord, don't you know all the loss I have sustained this year? Have you forgotten me? Have you forgotten what I have just gone through? What I am still going through? Not this, too! This is too much. I can't bear this loss of more family." I had been so very happy at the thought that my son was about to come home, live in Atlanta, have an occasional dinner at my house, and just be there. How could God rip this from me so unexpectedly?

Fortunately, I did not say any of this out loud. Houston went on to say, "This is the smartest group of people I have met through my interviews. They have a compelling product that I believe in. Two of my mentors have said that technology is an area they think is the place to be for a new college grad. This job will have me making presentations to CIOs and COOs and honing my communication skills at a very high level. I think I am going to accept their offer. What do you think?"

This would be my hardest test of doing the right thing as a mother. I knew that because of my son's respect for my business experience, I could perhaps influence his decision. I also knew that would be wrong. I could not say that I thought turning down an offer from a top tier investment firm to go to work for a 100-person tech company was a wise decision, but I could stop myself from discouraging him from pursuing this dream.

I said, "For the last few years, you have made excellent decisions about your future. You have worked hard in your internships, you have done your homework and research for your job search, and at this point you are probably better informed about what is best for you than I am. If I do the risk-reward matrix on the two jobs, they both have different things to offer. I will say that if you are ever going to make a mistake, now is the time. You are 23. If you go to California and this is not the lottery-ticket job you think it is, you can always come back and take a traditional job.

This is one decision you will have to make for yourself, and I will support you whatever you decide."

Houston was stunned. He said, "That is not at all what I thought you would say." That moment began a change in our relationship as he realized that I greatly respected his wisdom in making good decisions. It made him more open to consulting me and sharing with me about many more things in the future. That part of this story was good.

The personal loss I faced from my only son's move to California was the biggest loss of all to the life I had lived for so many years. While he was in college, my son being in my home every summer and for a month between each semester had made me not feel as if I lived alone. The frequent weekend visits had supported that illusion. There was no way I could delude myself any longer when he was living on the other side of the country. I knew that my friends' children who lived on the west coast certainly did not get home for both Thanksgiving and Christmas. Most adult children did not want to use most of their limited vacation time in their early careers flying home and experiencing jet lag. Life as I knew it was over. This was the third huge gaping hole blown in my life in a very short period of time. I felt my life was in shreds and very, very empty.

God takes lives in shreds and puts them together in beautiful but unexpected ways. I feared loneliness. For the next year, however, I would not have a minute for a lonely thought or a lonely day. Grief, yes, but I was too busy and too surrounded with people to be lonely.

Isaiah 43:19 says:

See, I am doing a new thing! Now it springs up; do you not perceive it? I am making a way in the wilderness and streams in the wasteland.

And that is what God did. He nourished me with streams of His love and more fellowship than I could even handle.

First, the church asked me to be one of three women to volunteer to lead Women's Ministry until a new director could be hired. We thought they meant four to six weeks; it was over a year! This role took thirty to forty hours of my time weekly for the first five months. Because our women always saw me walking the church halls with Belinda or sitting with her at church dinner, I became a visible and accessible go-to person for women to bring all kinds of ideas, needs, heartaches and prayer requests they would normally bring Belinda. It was a sweet, rich time of learning to know them more deeply and love them more deeply. Because women were grieving Belinda's loss, the Prayer Team I led became busier than usual. Our weekly prayer meetings had consisted of Belinda bringing in a list of prayer requests from the women in Bible studies or from members dropping by her office to confide in her. I found I needed to reach out to the Bible Study teachers so I would know them better and know the needs of the women in their classes. We even had some events occur that had never happened in the past. On several occasions, we had women walking in and asking to be prayed over on the spot in our meeting! God was doing a new thing!

When I got home each evening, my phone rang off the hook and my personal email was overflowing. Just responding to all these people took hours and was a delightful substitute to my nightly calls from Belinda or my chats with my sister.

And there were other perks. One of the most wonderful groups at our church is the Widow's Group. They say it is the one club you never want to join. Still, everyone knows that once you are part of that group, the luncheons and fellowship are among the loveliest, most fun activities in our community thanks to their wise and witty leader. Our church takes very seriously the exhortations in the Bible to care for widows, and we do it well. Once a month, they enjoy a speaker, a lovely luncheon after church, and many thoughtful touches from the Women's Ministry. Since I am not a widow, I could not attend; however, Marion, the beloved leader of the Widow's Group asked us as leaders to attend in Belinda's place as sponsor. This has been one of the most enjoyable social activities I have ever done, and the women are engaging, interesting, and fun. The love and consideration they show for each other was extended to me, and I found myself greatly looking forward to these monthly get-togethers.

In fact, every Sunday was filled up with an opportunity to have lunch with someone. Unless I chose to (because I would occasionally need a breather!), I never had to go home from church and be by myself!

And God surprised me through my much-loved son as well. First, he loved his new job, and we all want our children to be fulfilled in their careers. More importantly, God gave him the perfect Christian friend on the first day of his new job—what are the odds of that? These two had much in common, including both having just graduated from UNC, though they had not known each other.

The surprise was that Houston did come home for both Thanksgiving and Christmas! I had set my expectations low with him and God exceeded them! Also, because

Houston had to set up a brand new apartment and had nothing but the clothes he took with him, he included me in his apartment search and in shopping to furnish his new place. In my trip to San Jose before his first day of work, we bought everything from dishcloths (which he said he did not need) to a bed and sofa with the moving bonus the company had given him. We visited a wonderful church, which he attended most of his first year. When Houston needed to move later that year, he gladly accepted my offer for me to come out again and hang drapes and decorate his larger apartment. That first year as I was adjusting to my new life, I saw my west coast son far more than I would ever have dreamed.

I ended that difficult year in amazement at all God had done. Christian writer and speaker Jill Briscoe says we will all have moments when we want to ask God "why," when there seems to be no way what is going on in our lives will ever make sense. She says there are also corresponding moments, months or years later when we say, "Ahhh, so that's why that was."

While I was in my season of loss, I had looked at my life as a huge, dark empty void. I had little hope that anything would fill it or assuage my loneliness. Instead, that year brought me blessings overflowing. The quality time Houston and I spent getting him established in California yielded more rich conversations than any of my friends were having with their sons who lived near them. I had new friends, enriched friendships with old friends, and a sense of purpose and belonging in my church that was beyond anything I had experienced before. Colossians 2:6-7 says:

So then, just as you received Christ Jesus as Lord,
continue to live your lives in him, rooted and built up in him,

strengthened in the faith as you were taught, and
overflowing with thankfulness.

God did not send these losses to weaken me or deprive me. I grew that year and was more rooted and strengthened in Him than ever. I ended the year knowing that He had not forgotten me, but that He had blessed me more than I ever could have imagined. I ended the year with a thankful heart. Psalm 23:5 states;

> *You prepare a table before me in the presence of*
> *my enemies. You anoint my head with oil; my cup*
> *overflows.*

I truly felt my cup was overflowing, filling the gaping holes and emptiness I thought was my future.

My story reminds me of that of Hagar told in Genesis 15. Hagar's life was filled with difficult circumstances. She was an Egyptian who was taken to be the slave of Sarah, Abraham's wife. Living apart from her friends and family, she was badly mistreated by her mistress. She was kicked out while she was pregnant to fend for herself, all alone in the desert. This exile was a death sentence. She was desolate, but God sent an angel and He delivered God's encouragement and promises of all He would do for her in the future in a very personal way. He would use her difficult circumstances to bless her, and her soon-to-be-born son would one day give her a large family and a future. When Hagar understands that God has not forgotten her and plans to save her and bless her, she realizes His true character and how He cared for her:

She gave this name to the LORD who spoke to her: "You
are the God who sees me,' for she said, 'I have now seen
the One who sees me.' Genesis 15:13

How about you? Do you see no way out of a circumstance you are in? Do you feel lonely? Do you doubt that God sees the very details of your life and how difficult it is for you right now?

He is the God who sees you. More importantly, He wants to bless you and care for you in ways you may not be able to see right now. Continue to pray and read His Word so you will receive His guidance and comfort every day. Attend a Bible study so you can learn more of the promises God has for you. His promises never fail.

XIII. ❧ God Is With You in Your Work

When I look at my career, I don't think I have ever had a truly great idea. I have had some good ideas, but everything amazing that has taken my career to new levels has been the work of the Holy Spirit. Not only can I not take any credit, I have to admit to being balky at times and resistant to something that was going to prosper me and to give me a better future (Jeremiah 29:11.)

Even before I gave my life totally to the Lord, I know He had His eyes on me and was always trying to nudge me in the right direction. If you sometimes think you are feeling that still small voice, pray about it. God may be taking you in a new direction in order to bless you and use you in a way you could not foresee but He does. We often think that hearing from God is going to be accompanied by fireworks or emotionalism, but more often it is just a gentle drawing to what He wants you to do. Elijah wanted to see God, to hear from Him, and God revealed Himself to him. Here is what Elijah says in I Kings 19:12:

And after the earthquake a fire; but the Lord was not in the fire: and after the fire a still small voice. KJV

So the dazzling earthquake or fire did not contain God's voice; Elijah heard it in the stillness. I want to share with you some times in my life when God, through the Holy Spirit who works through us here on earth, led me to change my will and my direction.

Before I started my own consulting business, I spent some time as a consultant at a large international firm. Unlike today, female business consultants were rare. On a team of five to twenty men, I might be the only female. Even though I was a project manager and was teaching management principles in corporate seminars, because I was a female, I looked like a secretary to these men. At the end of a brainstorming meeting where many complex strategies were developed for our clients, the men would look over to me and say, "Casey, you write up the report." At that time, they had no idea I could write; I just was the right gender to be the secretary.

In those days I was pretty feisty and not hesitant to stand up for my rights, but something inside me told me to just write the reports and not fight. I will say the reports took a lot of time, and I wanted to complain about the injustice of it, but something (Someone) helped me hold my tongue. And then some interesting things started happening.

First, I began to be invited to important meetings that were way above my pay grade. As a project manager, there were project chiefs, managers, directors, and a host of other executives above me. I was invited to meetings that no other project managers were allowed to attend, even partners' meetings! The reason was that I held all the information on everyone else's projects because I had summarized their information for the reports. Partners found that it was efficient to have me there as I had a good overview of all the project managers' results and challenges. This recognition catapulted my career forward at an amazingly fast pace. I never saw that coming.

A second thing that happened was that the clients figured out that I could write reports. They would sometimes ask my superiors if I could help them write key documents such as business plans. First, I had to figure out what a business plan looked like! But I learned by working with some of the top decision makers in Fortune 500 companies; they gave me the ideas and I was their wordsmith. I was bringing in more work my company had not anticipated, and they loved it. The clients grew to trust me through this process, so when we needed to discuss money or other difficult subjects, my firm started sending me in to talk to C-level executives—long before my peers were ever allowed to meet with people at this level. By being willing to do the lowliest job that no one wanted to do, I was given bonuses and promotions. I could not believe that this very behind-the-scenes menial task led to great visibility. Only God could have come up with that one!

Later, when I started my own consulting firm, I had several niche specialties that few consultants could offer such as writing business plans, industrial sales proposals, and other documents my clients had taught me to write on the job. These have been my most lucrative skills and helped provide a comfortable income doing a job I did mostly from home while I was raising a child. My most popular seminar has been *Powerful Business Writing*, and when I needed the money most, this seminar grossed over $200,000 in one year.

Much of my early income came from Southern Company, especially the subsidiary Georgia Power that was practically in my backyard. These are the most ethical, family-oriented people you would ever want to work for, and working for them in my early years as a mom was a huge blessing. I did not land this wonderful client through brilliant marketing or good business strategies. God led me to do some things earlier in my career that did not seem to have any reward in it for me at the time, but that resulted in this blessing. Let me explain how God worked in this instance.

One of the jobs my husband wanted me to take after we got married was as a consultant at First National Bank of Atlanta, later Wachovia. I was very much opposed to taking this job, but my husband felt it was what I should do. I was trying to honor him as my husband, so I reluctantly took this job that paid less than what I was used to and seemed to offer nothing that delighted or interested me. One of the people on the job was Susan Wise, a very insightful, observant, and direct woman. The misery level at my house was high, and my husband went to his club and played cards and drank until very late many nights. If and when he did come home, the angry fighting was worse than I can describe. I did not want my friends to know about the hellish evenings we spent because I still had hopes we could work through the issues. At that time, I had no child to spend time with, so I would go to my parents to spend the evening if I knew his poker game was destined to be a late one.

My parents lived in Canton, Georgia about forty-five miles away, so about once a week I would drive up after work and spend the night with them instead of driving back so late. One day, someone at work who lived in Canton said something about the terrible traffic on I-575 that morning. I let slip that I had been in that traffic and agreed with this person.

A few days later, Susan made a comment to me about the problems in my marriage. I was a bit put off as I had carefully hidden my unhappiness. Susan and I were barely acquaintances then, and I was feeling very much the failure in my marriage. To complicate things, the president of the bank knew my husband from a business connection they had years ago, and it was critical that the bank think highly of my husband in hopes of any future business for my husband's commercial and industrial real estate business. I struggled to be polite and really wanted to deny what she had just said. Something prompted me to just ask questions and not retort the way my disposition made me want to reply. I asked her what led her to think that.

In her completely honest way, she said, "I was in my cubicle and overheard you were on I-575 yesterday morning. Your parents live in Canton, so I assumed you were coming from there at 7:00am. What newlywed goes to stay at her parents' house overnight in the first year of marriage? Sounded like trouble to me."

I was aghast. I am so hesitant to breach rules that I sometimes am not as open as Susan was, and when something like this happens, I can be a bit shocked. For a moment, I really did not like what she had said. Then I felt an immense relief. Susan did not know my friends or my husband's friends, so my husband would not be diminished in those circles by this disclosure. It was really a load off my shoulders to have someone I did not have to pretend with. She and her husband Roy were so kind to me. Then I got to know her extraordinarily kind and gifted daughters, and they remain a family I admire tremendously.

We parted ways after this bank job proved to be too rigid for me to be able to accommodate my husband's schedule, and he wanted me to try something more flexible and more lucrative. That is when I started the consulting practice. Susan left about the same time to join a small but prestigious consulting firm called Executive Speaker. We both had the skill set to teach writing and speaking, but we took different paths as we left the bank and sort of lost touch as we busily started new jobs.

A few months into my new entrepreneurial adventure, I received a call from one of the principals at Executive Speaker who had heard about me from Susan. I was asked if I did writing seminars. I said, "Yes, I am calling you from my break at Bellsouth where I am conducting one today."

I was told that Executive Speaker had a writing product, but that they did not handle industrial proposals and some of the more complex documents. Their client Georgia Power was shopping around and comparing consultants. Another firm that could handle both speaking and writing complex documents was threatening Executive Speaker's business. Executive Speaker made this offer: They would bring me in as a satellite associate to teach writing only. I could never solicit the speaking business from their client. I was also to pay them a finder's fee. I gladly accepted and we did business that way for over ten years. I am friends with these people to this day.

I did not win that great client because I was a skilled writer or a great presenter. God brought me that business because He hemmed me in that day from telling Susan that my business was not her business. He gave me that business because the relationship Susan and I developed caused her to go to the principals of Executive Speaker and say, "You can trust Casey not to go after our speaking business if she gets her foot in the door as a writing consultant."

I thought God was telling me not to be rude to Susan that day because He wanted me to be nice. He did, but He also wanted to bless me. So often, when we are obedient to do things we really don't want to do, we find later that God had a blessing in it for us, too.

And here is an interesting side note. Executive Speaker has a reputation for screening and interviewing associates for up to a year before entering into a contract with them. The fact that they signed me on-the-spot was largely due to Susan and the time pressure they were feeling. But I think what gave them the greatest confidence in me was that the day they called me, I had mentioned that I was on-site delivering a writing seminar to Bellsouth, a Fortune 500 company. The reason I was there was another example of how God would prompt me to do things that did not make any sense but that I felt compelled to do. Some people call this intuition. Often, it is the Holy Spirit nudging you. I have alluded to this time at Bellsouth earlier, but the way I came to be hired there in the first place is a story only God could have written.

I had agreed to start this consulting practice and was already terrified as I am not by nature an entrepreneur. But God blessed my business greatly, and I had clients literally from the first day. I had enough business but every consultant can use more. I received a call from a woman I had recommended for an internal job at Wachovia. This dear lady told me her husband was in charge of hiring technical trainers and speakers for Bellsouth. He was not the one in charge of management training, but he could perhaps put me in touch with someone who could hire me for some contract work. I was very excited! We met and my friend's husband vouched for me and got me an interview with the Manager of Management Training and Development. Bellsouth was such an admired company that I was thrilled to have this opportunity to pitch my services.

The interview went well, but I had made a critical mistake. I had not done my homework about what this company paid or what the job opening even was. It turns out that the job was facilitating someone else's video-based program. Because I was not delivering my own program and because I would be silent during the videos, this opening paid about a third of what I was being paid by other clients. When the manager told me the pay, I almost fell over. I initially just knew this was an emphatic "NO." But that still, small voice just would not let me say, "No." I asked questions so I could buy time to figure out why in the world I was not already walking out the door. The main reason I did not want to refuse it is that my friend's husband had really stuck his neck out for me. He had put forth a great deal of effort, and I didn't want to tell him he had wasted his time. I decided to do this video-based program with the hopes I could figure out how to sell them some of my programs that did not pay this almost insulting rate of pay.

But I did not know what God knew. God knew then that two days after I accepted these paltry wages, that I would find out I was pregnant. God could also foresee something that I could not: that mine would be a high-risk pregnancy and ordered to stay off my feet. I could never have done the higher paying seminar work I was used to in those critical months when the obstetrician thought I would lose my baby. I had no choice but to work since I had no other income, but the Bellsouth job was mostly sitting while a video did the presenting. It was the perfect job for me. And when I landed the Georgia Power job, they did not want to start until the first of the year, so I was able to do my cushy, comfortable video teaching until I had to stop working in the final month of my pregnancy. I knew in an instant why I had been prompted to accept wages that the other consultants who were my advisors told me would hurt my credibility in the market.

God knew and God had a plan. The Holy Spirit put a guard on my tongue and did not let me blurt out, "Thanks, but no thanks" when the shockingly low fee was offered to me. Here are some Biblical principles that played out in my life in that experience, even though I barely knew anything about the Bible at that time.

1. God truly took circumstances that did not look rewarding to me and worked them together for my good.

Romans 8:28 ESV

And we know that for those who love God all things work together for good, for those who are called according to his purpose.

2. Accepting the low fee violated one of my business practices of giving every client the same fair price. This practice kept my rates consistently high and avoided clients becoming angry if they found I was reducing my rate for someone. My way seemed so much wiser to me than God's way as I contemplated rejecting the offer in that office that day. But I have learned that God is so much smarter than I am.

Isaiah 55:8 ESV

For my thoughts are not your thoughts, neither are your ways my ways, declares the Lord.

And He can even outthink the wise:

1 Corinthians 1:27 NIV

But God hath chosen the foolish things of the world to confound the wise; and God hath chosen the weak things of the world to confound the things which are mighty;

3. God has one huge advantage over us: He can see the future. His Holy Spirit works inside our hearts to urge us to do things to prepare for future events we can't see coming. Obeying the promptings of the Holy Spirit is always in our best interest, though what we are asked to do may make no sense at the time.

John 16:13

When the Spirit of truth comes, he will guide you into all the truth, for he will not speak on his own authority, but whatever he hears he will speak, and he will declare to you the things that are to come.

4. I should never dig my heels in and be inflexible about what I plan to do and how I plan to do it without praying and asking God. It is at his pleasure and because of His mercy that I even wake to a new day and am alive. We may have definite plans based on what we know, but there is so much that we don't know about what can happen to our health, the economy, our families and so much more. We are operating with very limited information; God holds all the information for now and through eternity.

James 4:13-17

Come now, you who say, "Today or tomorrow we will go into such and such a town and spend a year there and trade and make a profit"— yet you do not know what tomorrow will bring. What is your life? For you are a mist that appears for a little time and then vanishes. Instead, you ought to say, "If the Lord wills, we will live and do this or that." As it is, you boast in your arrogance. All such boasting is evil. So whoever knows the right thing to do and fails to do it, for him it is sin.

5. God doesn't just know all about the world, He knows me. He knows me better than I know myself. Because He knows me truly and deeply, I can trust Him when He redirects my life, even though I may not like it at the time.

Psalm 139:16

Your eyes saw my unformed substance; in your book were written, every one of them, the days that were formed for me, when as yet there was none of them.

Psalm 90:2

Before the mountains were brought forth, or ever you had formed the earth and the world, from everlasting to everlasting you are God.

Do you make it a practice to stop before taking the next step in your life or career to say, "God, what do you think is a good idea?"

Do you ever have promptings or nudges such as the ones described in this chapter? Spend some time alone and seek to know if those promptings are the work of the Holy Spirit trying to lead you and guide you to the best choices and responses you can make. Remember, He is privy to the future and may know more than you do at this moment about what would best bless you for the rest of your life.

Do you pray before you make job decisions such as applying for new jobs, preparing for important meetings, and holding conversations with your employer or customers? You have the best advisor in the world. Pause to get His take on all things.

Facing the future with the help of the almighty God behind you is a powerful thing. Take time today to pray about one work-related relationship or financial decision or conversation. Ask God to show you what He would do. Then listen, really listen. Remember how we said that you will hear God in the still small voice? You will have to be still yourself if you want to hear the still small voice. Get very quiet after you pray and see if God nudges you. Spend some time in His Word and see if He has guidance for you there. God answers prayers in all kinds of ways. He will answer you in His way and in His time.

XIV. &❧ God Is With You When You Don't Know What to Do

We all have times when we simply don't know what to do next. Our lives at some juncture may lack clear direction and purpose. Getting up each morning and doing the daily things God wants us to do can lead us to that purpose though we may not even realize it. Being faithful in the small things can lead to big things. Small things include having a quiet time of Scripture reading and conversation with God before the day takes you into unknown situations and opportunities, being faithful in small service assignments God gives you, and remembering to thank and praise Him in all things.

Most of us wish we had a clear plan or road map that would tell us exactly what our next move should be. Only on rare occasions do we receive that kind of clear direction. Instead, God's plan usually unfolds in a slow and gentle way.

Circumstances may block what we thought was the plan for our day or year. We find ourselves having to regroup and redirect. What was on our agenda for the month may have been very clear and now may be wiped out, and we find ourselves asking, "What should I do now?"

This occurred for me when my consulting business hit a slow season, and I had some extra time on my hands. I knew I should do something to market, but instead I became enthralled with the idea of designing an internet-based program for grammar. Now this was a strange thing to get obsessed with because it was not the type of service my clients were buying. I taught employees to write proposals, reports, customer service emails, and other documents. Another odd thing was that this was in 1993, and e-learning was not a popular mode of corporate training, so why was I suddenly obsessed with a project like this? Still, I could not get it off my mind and indulged myself in pursuing this project. I sensed God had put this idea on my heart, but it made no sense. Still, I commenced working on my first e-learning project, even though I knew nothing about e-learning.

There were definitely bumps along the way. First, I had no idea how time consuming this type of design was. I had always lectured, and the design for that is very simple. Pages and pages of design went into the presentation of each idea in an e-learning module. Also, the format was very detailed and I am not a detail person, so the work was painstakingly slow for me.

What I thought would take a week or two began to stretch out for weeks and then months. I wanted so badly to quit, but I had invested hundreds of hours and felt I had to finish- even though I had no idea what I would do with this project when I finished. But business was a bit slow the month I started, so this project kept me busy. Even on days when I had no clients to serve, I could get up and go to my computer and feel productive.

I met with further discouragement trying to find a web-designer who would help me launch this project. I researched several and finally chose a man who was head of Internet services for a nearby college. I was very specific about the highly interactive, self-paced program I wanted, and he assured me he was experienced in designing the technical interface for programs like this. That turned out not to be true. After weeks of his failed attempts and losing a great deal of my money, it was evident he did not have the skills to help me. I was in my office just sick over losing my investment. I was kicking myself for throwing so much money away and for all of my lost time. As a consultant, time spent on anything is time I could not charge a client for. Business had picked up, and I did not want to think of the consulting dollars I had lost by trying to see this disaster through to the end.

Suddenly, I thought of a high school teacher I once knew who had told me of a couple of computer geniuses she had taught in her gifted class. At first I rejected the thought to call them, but then I thought, "They will probably charge so little that it would not be that much of a loss if they fail. Why not try?"

When I called, she said that one of the boys was now attending Georgia Tech. I called the student, Rob, and he eagerly said "yes" to meet me the next day. When we met, he was very professional and even had a proposal ready. He assured me that achieving the interactivity and instant student feedback I desired was easy for him. And he was right.

He created a product I used with virtually no changes for twenty years.

And here was something God knew that I didn't: this program really was a marketing tool. I had felt guilty for not working on my marketing when all along this e-learning would enhance my marketing more than anything else I could possibly do. In my field of consulting on business communication, the competition is plentiful. Time and time again over the next twenty years, the fact that I had interactive, self-paced e-learning as a value-add to my seminars differentiated me from my competitors. Clients loved the feeling of doing something new, and they appreciated that the learning went on for weeks after the seminar. I had not known why I had been so compelled to invest so much time and money in this project, but now I know that the Holy Spirit was prompting me in this direction.

In all my years in business, no other project has ever paid me back so richly or for so many years. It was meant for me to get up each day and chip away at that project for so long. Staying in the habit of going to work each day, even if this project was speculative, was exactly what I was supposed to have done. I did not have a clear vision of the ultimate purpose, but God did.

A few years later, I took on another task that did not seem to make sense at the time. I had been having hip and back problems, and standing on my feet all day was becoming increasingly difficult. My primary source of revenue was from a seminar that required that I stand for the better part of two days to lecture, and I was often in great pain afterwards. Also, I was developing tears in my knees and had an upcoming surgery scheduled.

The stress of health problems was complicated by having a sixteen year old in the house who was going through his most unpleasant stage ever. It was hard for us to communicate for very long most days without one of us bristling. I knew it was temporary, but it seemed to last an agonizingly long period of time.

On the morning of my surgery, I was waiting downstairs in my living room very early, waiting for my faithful friend Luanne to come pick me up and take me to the surgical center. I prayed to God and said, "Lord, I need help. I don't know how much longer I am going to be able to stand and do these all-day seminars, but I don't know what else to do for a living. And I don't know what to do with my son; we love each other so much, but we are making each other so unhappy. I am going to place all of this in your hands because I have tried and tried to figure out what to do and I just can't."

As soon as I prayed, peace flooded my soul. I knew things would be alright.

A few minutes later, the director of the business communication department of Georgia State University called me. After a friendly chat about how she knew of my credentials, she offered me an adjunct position teaching just one course, one night a week. When she told me how little it paid, I initially declined as politely as I could.

As soon as I did, conviction flooded my thoughts. I remembered that long ago I had said I would like to teach a class of young people in order to give back to my community. God also planted in my mind that this class could be the door opening to a new career teaching at a university where I could even do my teaching from a wheelchair if need be. The seminar business preferred young, physically vibrant people, but a university was very accommodating to people with disabilities. I recoiled at this at first. I would have to teach for a month to earn what the seminars paid in two days. Still, I realized that I had prayed and God had given me an answer. Just because I did not like His answer did not mean I should turn it down. I picked the receiver up, called the director back, and agreed to teach the course.

God had set a plan in motion to care for me that did not seem as valuable to me then as I know it is now. The one course developed into a full-time faculty position. I could sit on a stool or at a desk while I lectured. After ten years of teaching, I earned a pension. Since I had experienced such financial setbacks at forty, I really needed this pension as I had provided well for my child but not for myself. More importantly, I saw very quickly that this assignment was not just about teaching and a paycheck: it was a mission. God had sent me to serve many urban and international students who desperately needed to be prepared for the job market. The course I taught included topics such as ethics, values, and interpersonal skills, and I could help them develop those. More importantly, when appropriate, I got to live out my Christian values in front of them and perhaps provoke thought and interest in them about their beliefs and eternal disposition.

I am so grateful that the Holy Spirit prompted me to call the director back that day and agree to teach that course that has resulted in so many blessings.

The final example of God telling me what to do when I had no idea what to do concerned my beloved sister Jan. At an early age, Jan was selected to attend an experimental kindergarten for extremely gifted children. Her intellect was phenomenal. She played seven musical instruments brilliantly by the time she finished elementary school. She was an artist, painting in oils and creating beautiful jewelry she designed herself.

Jan was also bipolar and an alcoholic. Conversations with her could be the most entertaining and fascinating times of my life, or they could be some of the most painful and fearful times of my life. She could be kinder and more thoughtful of me than anyone I had ever known, but I never knew when she might come at me in anger, even physically. Though we loved each other and spent a lot of time together off and on throughout the years, Jan would occasionally turn on me for no reason and her hatred would be white-hot. These episodes were unprovoked and irrational, so I never knew what I was walking into when I met with her. My parents had depleted their retirement paying for at least nine rehab programs or psychiatric hospitals as her very public problems continued to erupt into her forties and fifties. We had all tried everything.

Jan loved her son so much I cannot describe the intensity of it, but she could not stop drinking. I was with her in the hospital that first night of his precious life, and I went home with her from the hospital and stayed the first night. My sister Bobbi and other friends stayed the next few nights. As soon as Jan was alone, she began drinking again. I would try to support her with friendship, babysitting, financial help, and Christian materials and experiences. Nothing could stop her binge drinking. She eventually lost her child to DFACS, and Bobbi and her husband raised him to be a fantastic young Christian man, one of God's most incredible works. Still, Jan never got over this heartache.

I can't describe how losing my hope that Jan would change affected me. I was eight years older than Jan, and because my mother was sometimes hospitalized and fragile herself, I was almost like a parent to Jan when we were growing up. I felt like such a failure that I could not reason her into giving up her drinking to attain the custody of her child that she so desperately wanted. At some point, I knew that I could not do anything further to help her. I prayed and the Lord was very clear to me what I was to do: I was to love her. That does not sound like very much of a game plan, does it? I wanted a plan with a result at the end that merited white chips and a stable life. But that was never to be for Jan.

After the Lord told me that my job in Jan's life was not to improve her or heal her or guide her but just to love her, I had perfect peace. Before, I felt that if I were loving to Jan while I knew she was living an unhealthy lifestyle that I was enabling or not showing tough love. After this conversation with God, I felt free just to love her.

It was not easy as she was sometimes not an easy person to deal with, but I could persevere, as this was a mission from God. He showed me that He had loved me when I was unlovable and doing things that He said were not right. I was no better than Jan, yet He valued both of us. He also showed me that loving and serving Jan was the best opportunity I would ever have to love as Christ loves. I would never receive anything in return and I would have to turn the other cheek after many a cursing out or a berating for something I did not do, but my love for her was not based on quid pro quo. I loved her unconditionally just as God had loved me unconditionally.

I loved Jan until she died of cancer in 2013. I loved her through treatment and through good times and bad. We had times of deep fellowship and times when she refused to speak to me, but she always knew I loved her. When DFACS took her to court to take her son away, I was not allowed in the courtroom for one of the sessions. I was told that the DFACS attorney was being brutal. He said to her while she was on the stand (paraphrasing), "Isn't it true that you have been unable to form positive relationships with anyone, that you have no support system because of your combative actions? You do not have a good relationship with neighbors, you cannot hold a job, and you have no relationship with anyone in your family."

I was told that Jan broke down weeping then and in a strangled cry said, "I know my sister Casey loves me."

And she was right. I sometimes fail in the things God wants me to do, but I loved Jan consistently and well in her most difficult years. That may not seem like a specific purpose or direction, but it was the one God assigned me, and it gives me peace to know that I did not fail Him or her.

Is there something God may be wanting you to do? It may be a career related task like my e-learning project or it might be to love a family member or neighbor unconditionally. Pray for His direction in your life. Does He have a purpose He wants to be fulfilled? Don't be surprised if what He guides your heart to is not glamorous or fun. Isaiah 55:8 says:

""For my thoughts are not your thoughts, neither are your ways my ways," declares the LORD."

No truer words were ever written. God's ways can be so unexpected and mystifying at first, but He is always right.

The blessing will be in your obedience to Him.

CONCLUSION ॐ

God has written my story and He is at this moment writing yours. Won't you give Him a chance to take you on this incredible adventure called Christianity? With the power of God behind you and the comfort and help of the Holy Spirit guiding your steps for the future, you can experience a type of fearless living that is exhilarating.

Pray today that God will reveal Himself to you in some way and that He will open the next door for you in your journey to know Him better. Just talk to Him as you would to any friend you were wanting to get to know better. He loves you, and it is a conversation He has been longing for you to start.

About the Author

Casey Hawley resides in Atlanta and currently teaches the course Business Communication and Professionalism at Georgia State University. She consults on business writing and other communication and career topics for clients as diverse as the Department of the Interior, the NFL, many Fortune 100 companies, and mid-size technology companies.

Casey was moved to write this book when the Holy Spirit repeatedly brought to her mind the story of the nine lepers from Luke 17:12-19. Originally, this book was never meant to be published. It was a private acknowledgment to God for all He had done for her, a thank you from the author to her Lord and Savior.

Casey also speaks to women's groups about the topics covered in this book and other Christian topics including brokenness, communication, tithing, the Light of life, a grateful heart, single-parenting, and prayer. She can be contacted at ChristianityAdventures@gmail.com.

Author's note: I have recalled dates of the events in this book to the best of my ability. Still, I apologize in advance if there are any discrepancies.

A.

Adventures in Christianity: Lessons in Fearless Living
through an Unfailing God! Who says it is not exciting
to be a Christian?

by Casey Hawley

If this book has touched your life, please leave a message at
ChristianityAdventures@gmail.com

Made in the USA
Lexington, KY
27 July 2017